Great Salsas

by the **BOSS** OF SAUCE

From the Southwest & Points Beyond

By W.C. Longacre,
Chef/Owner of W.C.'s Mountain Road Cafe
and Dave DeWitt, the Pope of Peppers

THE CROSSING PRESS
FREEDOM, CALIFORNIA

Books by Dave DeWitt

The Hot Sauce Bible (with Chuck Evans)
Meltdown (with Mary Jane Wilan)
Fiery Appetizers (with Nancy Gerlach)
Heat Wave (with Nancy Gerlach)

Copyright © 1997 by W.C. Longacre and Dave DeWitt
Cover and interior design by Victoria May
Front cover and back cover (bottom right) photographs by Eduardo Fuss
Cover texture by Jill Stutzman
Interior and back cover (top right) photographs courtesy of W.C. Longacre and
    Dave DeWitt
Printed in the U.S.A.

For information on bulk purchases or group discounts for this and other Crossing Press titles, please contact our Special Sales Manager at 800-777-1048.

ISBN 0-89594-817-6

In lⱺving memⱺry of Clyde, Martha, and Eric Longacre—with great appreciation for their nurturing love of food: from ethnic markets and corner bakeries, to diners and fine dining establishments, to home organic gardens, wildcrafting, and the bounty of land and sea.

Acknowledgments:

Kris Alberty,

Ileah Baylor,

Suzy Q Baylor,

Jeanette DeAnda,

Tammy Smart

Special thanks to

Martha Doster for

allowing our house to double

as an all-night test kitchen!

Contents

W.C. and Dave

W. C. Longacre

is a true adventurer. Born a maverick, he had to be tamed, or to put it more politely, molded by his mentors. When it comes to cooking, he is a natural with great integrity—a forager of wild herbs and mushrooms, a fisherman who either

eats his catch or smokes it for future meals. He is not a snob. The menu at his cafe is divided into meat dishes and vegetarian dishes. He can cook simple, and he can cook sophisticated. In short, he has integrity as a chef and as a human being.

W.C. with Alice Watson

W.C.'s Story...

My family's diverse tastes and dietary needs led me to design my first restaurant to accommodate anybody. I lived with a vegetarian, my mother was diabetic, my brother had a lot of allergies, my father was a meat and potatoes kind of guy, and I'd eat anything...Needless to say, going out to eat was a real hassle, so we ate at home, where I learned how to make everyone happy under one roof. My restaurant offered organic meat, as well as vegetarian fare; every table was set with raw honey and white sugar. You could have natural soda pop or Coca-Cola. After all, learning to please everyone is key to a good restaurant.

One of my first mentors was a Navajo woman, Alice Watson. One of life's funny circumstances brought us together and we adopted each other as grandmother and grandson. She taught me the Navajo way with stews and such.

I was a fairly accomplished home cook, but had no experience in a restaurant kitchen. I knew a third-generation Parisian chef, Rene, who had run several fine restaurants in France and the U.S. He hired me and taught me how to use a recipe and how to run a kitchen. I've never seen a person with more economy of movement. I learned a lot from him.

W.C. with Rene Cagnat

Dick Schmitz, a second-generation German restauranteur, taught me the etiquette and ethic of a chef. You didn't get creative in his kitchen; his was strictly by-the-book East Coast/European cuisine.

Dick Schmitz

As for the business side of running a restaurant, Matthew Ebenezer was my first teacher. Using the GI Bill from his time in Korea, he started in the Chicago ghetto and worked his way up to be the owner of a chain of rib huts in the midwest. I saw him dealing with all kinds of people, from the mayor and politicians to street people. It was his spicy food that first attracted me to him, but the most valuable lesson he taught me was to keep my eye on the till.

I encountered Shudi Cheong in Hong Kong. School in the Far East was not like school here. You were never shown anything twice. If you had a question, you were expected to ask it during the demonstration, not later. Six months later if you were called on to prepare a certain dish you were expected to know it and get it exactly right. From this I learned discipline.

W.C. with Matthew Ebenezer

In Dave DeWitt I have found a true culinary companion. We both really like fresh, inventive food. We fish together and we forage together, we tramp the canyon lands and trek up into the mountains where we hit the little lakes. Whenever possible, we use indigenous food such as blue corn-meal, grown and ground by Native Americans. We grow and smoke our own chiles. We get as close to the food chain as we can, gathering herbs, mushrooms, and wild berries, some of which grow only in this area.

W.C. with Shudi Cheong

Dubbed the Pope of Peppers,

Dave DeWitt has become the foremost authority on chile peppers in the world.

DeWitt caught the fiery fever upon moving to New Mexico where he discovered a culture that worships the holy capsicum. "Every late summer most families, Hispanic, Anglo, Indian, or Black, bought forty pounds of New Mexico green chiles, roasted and peeled them, and put them in the freezer hopefully to last for a year," DeWitt explains. "So I started to master as many New Mexican cooking techniques as I could, and soon I could make a red chile sauce that could compete with any."

Dave grilling at home in Albuquerque

Currently DeWitt is the president of Sunbelt Shows, Inc., which produces the National Fiery Foods Show, and publishes *Fiery Foods* magazine. He is the author or co-author of sixteen books extolling the mighty pepper.

Dave's Story...

When I was eight, my father and mother made the decision that whoever cooked didn't have to wash the dishes and thus my cooking career was launched. Later I began researching chiles in libraries all over the Southwest. I

Dave signing books with Paul Prudhomme

also interviewed growers and researchers, and collected clippings from newspapers and magazines. Soon I was publishing articles in numerous magazines. In the early '80s, I teamed up with Nancy Gerlach to write *The Fiery Cuisines,* a book about international chile cooking. Nancy and I went on to found *Chile Pepper* magazine and write many more books together.

During this time I began my first serious growing efforts. It was another aspect of chile information I had to master. I wanted to learn how to grow as many different varieties as I could.

I continue to grow exotic peppers from seeds that I have collected from all over the world. I utilize a greenhouse, and a medium-sized garden to grow such unusual varieties as 'Fatalii' from the Central African Republic, 'Congo Pepper' from Trinidad, 'Malagueta' from Brazil, and 'Rocotillo' from the Cayman Islands.

Dave in wholesale market in Bangkok

My gardening efforts produced so many chile pods that I began giving my exotic pods to the best chile chef I knew, W.C. Longacre, who not only created recipes for them, but tested them on all his customers. I love working with chefs, even if it's just providing some of the ingredients, and with a good friend and fellow chilehead like W.C., it's been a great collaboration.

Besides eating at W.C.'s Mountain Road Cafe, I enjoy walking through the "show and tell" chile garden of my friend Dr. Paul Bosland at New Mexico State University, haunting the stacks of university libraries to discover a new factoid about chile peppers, and traveling to exotic places with my wife—and of course, collecting chile seed on the trip!

Dave in Chile Demonstration Garden

Traditional Southwestern/Mexican patron saint of the kitchen, painted by nationally-known artist, Steve Reyes, as a gift to the cafe.

Introduction

We should begin by defining the word salsa. Many cookbooks define salsas as uncooked and sauces as cooked, but this distinction is not true in Mexico, where a salsa is simply a sauce. So when we use the term salsa, we mean literally any sauce that contains uncooked or cooked chile peppers of any consistency.

If Mexico is the mother of salsas, then the Southwest is the new muse of the salsa-making art. Thanks in part to creative chefs in Southwestern restaurants, salsas have reached new levels of creativity and taste. There is more happening here with salsas than anywhere else in the world. After all, San Antonio was the home of the first commercial salsa in the U.S., Pace Picante Sauce, which dates back to the 1950s. Interestingly enough, Albuquerque was the home of one of the first gourmet salsas, Territorial House, which eventually was purchased by Pace.

It is not surprising that Dave would team up with W.C., a chef who has made salsa the lifeblood of his Albuquerque restaurant, W.C.'s Mountain Road Cafe. Their collaboration actually began on a fishing trip when they both caught their limit of large striped bass. W.C. smoked the fish and prepared several salsas to accompany them. One thing led to another and soon Dave was growing exotic chiles such as rocotos, Trinidad seasoning peppers, *fatalii* habaneros, and yellow Thais, and dropping them off at W.C.'s restaurant where they would be incorporated into new salsas. And we mean new!

Because W.C.'s training as a chef took him to the Caribbean and Hong Kong, there are heavy tropical and Asian influences observable in his cooking. Some people might be surprised to find Asian style salsas in the Southwest, but salsa-making is continually evolving.

As Americans switch from the era of ketchup to salsa, we make a great culinary leap forward. However, as many commercial ketchups on the market are mediocre, so are many commercial salsas. Cooks who make their own salsas are taking a step in the right direction. Homemade salsas catch the eye and perk the palate. They are also good for the system. They are alternatives to heavy fat-laden, dairy-based foods that Americans are too dependent on. Salsas are a good way to diet without feeling as if you've sacrificed.

Now, for a hard-core salsa question: how hot should it be? W.C. suggests that it should be exactly as hot as you think it should be—you must taste as you go. If the recipe is too mild, obviously add more chiles. If it is too hot, dilute it with more of the main ingredients. The heat level should be adjusted to your comfort.

CHAPTER 1

THE Chile LEGACY OF New Mexico

We begin

our Southwest salsa search in New Mexico, not only because we live and work here, but because New Mexico has the oldest tradition of salsas of any state in the Southwest. Shortly after the first Spanish settlers founded Santa Fe around 1600, chile peppers were introduced into the region from Mexico. Thus began New Mexico's love affair with the pods that are the basis of red and green chile sauces, the foundation of the cuisine. These are the sauces that are ladled over enchiladas, burritos, tamales, beans, and virtually every other main dish. It's a 400-year-old tradition that's still going strong. As W.C. puts it, a real chilehead will walk into his restaurant and order a bowl of his red chile sauce and eat it like a soup!

In Albuquerque, Dave has his greenhouse and garden, where he grows every unusual variety of chile pepper he can get his hands on. After they are photographed, they are passed on to W.C. so that he can create recipes. Of course, his customers at the Mountain Road Cafe love projects like this because they get to taste the works in progress.

We're also fortunate that Albuquerque is the home of the National Fiery Foods Show, an extravaganza that gives us a chance to taste most of the new salsas released each year by manufacturers from all over the world. We're continually amazed not only by the number of new salsas and hot sauces, but also by their variety.

Our New Mexican salsas start with two of W.C.'s staples at the Mountain Road Cafe. W.C.'s Cafe Salsa is "a classic salsa fresca," as he puts it, hand-chopped with a very fresh taste. W.C.'s Chipotle Salsa is a puréed salsa, but he leaves some chunks in it. He says he can tell which waitperson is on duty by the salsas on their tickets, since they each have their own favorite one, which they suggest to the guests.

For enchiladas and burritos, W.C.'s Chimayó Red Chile Sauce is a staple at the Cafe, while Dave's Fresh Red Chile Sauce is made with fresh red chiles from his garden and is used in his home. Another staple Cafe sauce is W.C.'s Green Chile Sauce, a recipe that dates back more than twenty years.

Green Chile-Piñon Salsa contains two of New Mexico's most famous crops-although the piñon nuts are harvested in the wild rather than being cultivated like chile. Mushrooms grow wild in New Mexico. They are used in Wild Mushroom Chipotle Salsa.

New Mexico Firecracker Salsa is interesting because it's so simple to make with finely ground red chile powder. Roasting or grilling jalapeños before using them in salsas started in the northern states of Mexico. See our Roasted Jalapeño and Avocado Salsa and Grilled New Mexican Salsa.

Rio Grande Rainbow Salsa is a colorful, fresh salsa utilizing three chiles and a mango, while Roasted Corn and Poblano Chile Salsa reflects a 400-year culinary history of combining corn and chiles. Yellow Tomato Salsa with Red Habaneros offers another riot of colors and flavors. The fruity New Mexican Quincendental Hot Salsa is unique because we don't often find any recipe these days that utilizes quinces.

New Mexican chiles are hung in long strings, or "ristras." Then, they are rehydrated and combined with onions, garlic, oil, spices, and water to make the classic New Mexican red chile sauce, a common topping for enchiladas. The guajillos, a shortened and hotter version of the New Mexican chiles, are commonly used in sauces in northern Mexico.

W.C.'s CAFE SALSA

This is a foundation Southwest salsa, one used as a basis for other sauces in this book. It is also simply served with chips at the Cafe. It is very simple to put together. W.C. notes that it is not true that fresh is always better. In the case of tomatoes, market tomatoes often are not ripe, while canned puréed tomatoes are made from tomatoes that are too ripe to ship and therefore are flavorful and sweet. This particular salsa was a statewide award winner in the KOB-TV Restaurant Salsa Challenge, held in 1995. This recipe makes enough salsa for a party, and will keep for about a week in the refrigerator.

> 1/4 cup chopped fresh jalapeño chiles
>
> 3/4 cup chopped onion
>
> 1/2 tablespoon red wine vinegar
>
> 1/2 tablespoon minced garlic
>
> 1/2 tablespoon salt
>
> 1/2 tablespoon dried oregano leaf
>
> 3 cups tomatoes in heavy purée (about 3 quarts)

In a large bowl, combine the chiles, onion, vinegar, garlic, salt, and oregano. Mix thoroughly with a whisk. Add the tomato purée and mix thoroughly with a spoon. Allow to sit for about 2 hours to blend the flavors.

YIELD: ABOUT 1 QUART   HEAT SCALE: MEDIUM

W.C.'s Chipotle SALSA

This is one of the three basic salsas served at the Mountain Road Cafe, along with Cafe Salsa (p. 18) and Way South Salsa (p.75). It is generally served as a dip with chips, but W.C. suggests spreading it over a grilled chicken breast on a bolillo roll, topping it with grated mozzarella cheese and popping it under the broiler. A killer sandwich! This salsa will keep for 2 weeks in the refrigerator.

3 dried chipotle chiles, stems removed, rehydrated in hot water for about 20 minutes, then chopped

1 cup chopped roasted, peeled fresh New Mexican chile

2 cups canned puréed tomatoes

1 teaspoon salt

1 tablespoon sugar

2 fresh jalapeño chiles, seeds and stems removed, chopped

2 cloves garlic, chopped

1 teaspoon granulated garlic

1 teaspoon Old Bay seasoning

1 teaspoon honey

1 teaspoon toasted sesame oil

1 teaspoon dried Mexican oregano

1 tablespoon Smoky Hot Texas BBQ Sauce (see recipe, p. 47)

Combine, in batches, all the ingredients in a food processor and pulse until the mixture is coarse with small chunks. Allow to stand at room temperature for about 30 minutes to blend all the flavors.

YIELD: ABOUT 1 QUART   HEAT SCALE: HOT

There are four main large peppers used as the base for sauces: ancho, pasilla, New Mexican, and guajillo. The ancho is a wide, dark pepper with a "raisiny" aroma. It is the only pepper that is commonly stuffed in its dried form (the pod is softened in water first). The pasilla is a long, thin, dark pepper that also has a "raisiny" or nutty aroma. Along with the ancho, it commonly appears in Mexican "mole" sauces.

W.C.'S Chimayó RED CHILE SAUCE

Even in the heart of chileland in Albuquerque, W.C. is famous for this red chile sauce that is served over burritos and other New Mexican entrees. The key is the rich, high-impact chicken stock that is made in the style of classic French poaching stocks, with plenty of herbs. W.C. uses Chimayó chile in this recipe, a flavorful variety from northern New Mexico with a brilliant red-orange color. This sauce will keep for 3 days in the refrigerator.

1 tablespoon vegetable oil, soy preferred

2 cloves garlic

1/4 medium onion, chopped

1/2 teaspoon dried thyme

1 tablespoon Baker's baking chocolate, coarsely chopped

1 teaspoon salt

6 ounces ground red New Mexican chile,
Chimayó preferred

3 cups W.C.'s Chicken Stock (see recipe, p. 102)

1 cup water

In a food processor, combine the oil, garlic, onion, thyme, chocolate, and salt and purée to a coarse paste. Transfer to a bowl, add the ground red chile and mix. In a large pot, heat the chicken stock to boiling. Add the paste and boil for 10 minutes, stirring occasionally. Add the water and boil for 5 minutes or longer, until the desired consistency is reached, stirring constantly.

YIELD: ABOUT 1 QUART   HEAT SCALE: MEDIUM

DAVE'S Fresh Red CHILE SAUCE

This method of making chile sauce differs from other recipes that use fresh New Mexican chiles—they aren't roasted and peeled first. Because of the high sugar content of fresh red chiles, this sauce is sweeter than most. Dave harvested some chiles from his garden one late summer day, made a batch of this sauce, and ate every drop as a soup! It makes a tasty enchilada sauce, too. This sauce will keep for 3 days in the refrigerator.

1/4 cup vegetable oil

8 or more (to taste) fresh red New Mexican chiles, seeds and stems removed, chopped

1 large onion, chopped

3 cloves garlic

4 cups water

1/4 teaspoon ground cumin

1 tablespoon minced fresh cilantro

1/2 teaspoon dried Mexican oregano

Salt to taste

Heat the oil in a large saucepan and sauté the chiles, onion, and garlic until the onion is soft, about 7 minutes. Add the remaining ingredients, bring to a boil, then reduce the heat and simmer for 1 hour, uncovered. In a blender, purée the sauce in batches and return it to the saucepan. Cook until the sauce thickens to the desired consistency. Add salt to taste.

YIELD: ABOUT 3 CUPS   HEAT SCALE: MILD TO MEDIUM

Favorite Entrée Uses for Homemade Hot Sauce:

- *The perfect addition to a last minute quesadilla, one that is made only from ingredients in your larder and refrigerator.*

- *Transform canned soups into chilehead delights with a tablespoon or two.*

- *Mix with mayonnaise for that perfect sandwich spread.*

- *Pizza topping, anyone?*

- *Plain white rice takes on another dimension when mixed and heated with Asian hot sauces for an instant lunch.*

W.C.'S Green Chile SAUCE

This recipe dates to 1976, when W.C. created it for his first restaurant, the Morning Glory Cafe. It is meatless and dairyless, but "designed for a meat-eater's taste," according to W.C. It is easily frozen or canned. It will keep for 1 week in the refrigerator.

2 cups chopped New Mexican fresh green chiles

1/2 clove garlic, minced

1/4 medium onion, coarsely chopped

1/8 teaspoon ground coriander

1/2 teaspoon ground red chile powder

1/4 teaspoon white pepper

1/4 teaspoon ground cumin

1 teaspoon salt

3 cups water

2 teaspoons cornstarch

1 1/2 cups water

In a large pan, combine the green chile, garlic, onion, coriander, red chile powder, white pepper, cumin, salt, and water. Bring to a boil and boil, uncovered, for 1 hour. In a small bowl, combine the cornstarch and water and mix thoroughly. Add to the chile mixture and cook until the mixture clears, about 20 minutes.

YIELD: ABOUT 1 QUART   HEAT SCALE: MEDIUM

GREEN Chile-Piñon SALSA

We really love this salsa that captures two dominant flavors of New Mexican cuisine, chiles and piñon nuts. It is also great made with fresh red chile, which imparts a sweeter taste. It can be served as a dip or brushed on grilled meats or poultry. This recipe will keep 3-4 days in the refrigerator.

Blistering or roasting chiles is the process of heating the chile to the point that the tough transparent skin is separated from the meat of the chile so it can be removed. The method is quite simple.

6 fresh New Mexican green chiles, roasted, peeled, seeds and stems removed, chopped

4 tomatoes, peeled, seeded, and chopped

1/2 cup piñon nuts, lightly toasted in a dry saucepan

1/4 cup virgin olive oil

2 tablespoons balsamic vinegar

3 tablespoons fresh lime juice

3 scallions, chopped

3 tablespoons chopped fresh cilantro

2 cloves roasted garlic, chopped

Salt to taste

Combine all ingredients and allow to sit at room temperature for at least 1 hour to blend the flavors.

YIELD: ABOUT 4 CUPS   HEAT SCALE: MILD

Wild Mushroom
CHIPOTLE SALSA

A favorite dried chile pepper is the chipotle, a smoke–dried red jalapeño that has a fiery, smoky flavor. It is available loose in the dried form, or canned in adobo sauce. The latter is easier to use, because it's already rehydrated. To rehydrate the dried chipotles, simply soak them in hot water or any liquid, for an hour or more, depending on desired flavor.

During the summer, W.C. often wanders off to his favorite mountain hide-aways to collect morels, boletes, chanterelles, and black chanterelles for this salsa that he loves to serve over fish entrees. If fresh wild mushrooms are not available, rehydrate dried ones. This will keep for 1 week in the refrigerator.

2 medium dried ancho chiles, seeds and stems removed, chopped fine

1 cup water

8 dried chipotle chiles

1 cup water

1 cup wild mushrooms, chopped fine

3/4 cup balsamic vinegar

1 large shallot, minced

3 tablespoons extra virgin olive oil

1 cup dry white wine (Pinot Grigio preferred)

1 bottle Negra Modelo beer (or any dark beer)

Combine the ancho chiles and 1 cup water. Combine the chipotles and 1 cup water. Let the chiles rehydrate for 1 hour, then drain. Remove the seeds and stems from the chipotles and chop fine. In a saucepan, combine the chiles, mushrooms, vinegar, shallot and boil for 5 minutes. Remove from the heat, add the wine and beer, mix well and let stand for 2 hours. Serve at room temperature.

YIELD: ABOUT 3 CUPS   HEAT SCALE: HOT

NEW MEXICO Firecracker SALSA

Here is a quick, simple salsa for everyday use–W.C. says that it's not a celebration salsa, just a basic one. Although it's great as a dip, expand the culinary horizon by serving it on hamburgers or over eggs. This will keep for 3 days in the refrigerator.

3/4 cup ground Chimayó red chile

1 cup boiling water

1 tablespoon red wine vinegar

1/4 cup extra virgin olive oil

1 tablespoon Mexican oregano

3 cloves garlic, minced

1 cup Classic Chicken Stock (see recipe, p. 102)

1/2 cup chopped onion

6 medium Roma tomatoes, chopped

1 teaspoon salt

1 teaspoon sugar

In a bowl, combine the red chile and the boiling water, mixing well and avoiding inhalation of fumes. In a blender or food processor, combine the vinegar, olive oil, oregano, garlic, and chicken stock and purée. Combine the red chile mixture, puréed mixture, and the remaining ingredients in a bowl and mix well. Refrigerate for 2 hours before serving.

YIELD: ABOUT 3 CUPS   HEAT SCALE: HOT

ROASTED Jalapeño AND Avocado SALSA

Try this salsa over your morning omelet, or with grilled fish or chicken. It can also be made with fresh New Mexican green chile or even habaneros. The *garam masala* used here is a spice mixture available in Asian markets. This will keep for about a week in the refrigerator.

6 jumbo fresh jalapeño chiles, roasted over a flame and peeled, stems and seeds removed

4 red bell peppers, roasted over a flame and peeled, stems and seeds removed

3 avocados, pitted and peeled

2 cups chopped fresh cilantro

3/4 cup chopped fresh parsley

1/4 cup freshly squeezed lime juice, Key lime preferred

3 cloves garlic

3/4 teaspoon *garam masala*, or substitute imported curry powder

Pinch salt

Pinch sugar

Dice the jalapeños and bell peppers into 1/4-inch pieces. Combine the remaining ingredients in a food processor and process into a smooth paste. Remove to a bowl and stir in the jalapeños and bell peppers.

YIELD: ABOUT 3 CUPS   HEAT SCALE: HOT

Grilled NEW MEXICAN SALSA

Here's another salsa that's partially cooked. This is an all-purpose salsa that can be served with tortilla chips, enchiladas, tacos, as an accompaniment to grilled entrees, as well as an ingredient in other salsa recipes. This recipe will keep for about 3 days in the refrigerator.

- 6 fresh green New Mexican chiles
- 4 fresh jalapeño chiles
- 2 large tomatoes
- 4 tomatillos
- 2 medium onions, peeled
- 3 cloves garlic, minced
- 1/4 cup chopped fresh cilantro

Make a wood or charcoal fire and let it burn down to coals. Place the New Mexican chiles, jalapeños, tomatoes, tomatillos, and onions on a grill only a few inches above the coals. Grill the vegetables until the skins burn and pop, turning occasionally. Peel the vegetables, removing the stems and seeds from the chiles, and chop coarsely. Add the garlic and cilantro, mix well, and serve.

YIELD: ABOUT 2 CUPS   HEAT SCALE: HOT

Before roasting chiles, cut a small slit close to the top so that the steam can escape. The chiles can then be placed on a baking sheet and put directly under the broiler or on a screen on the top of the stove. Our favorite method is to place the pods on a charcoal grill about 5 to 6 inches from the coals. Blisters will soon indicate that the skin is separating, but be sure that the chiles are blistered all over or they will not peel properly. Immediately wrap the chiles in damp towels or place in a plastic bag for ten to fifteen minutes—this "steams" them and loosens the skins.

RIO GRANDE Rainbow SALSA

Handy Tools for Sauce

Making and Storage:

- *A large-mouth canning funnel*

- *The heaviest duty zip bags*

- *The sharpest knife you can*

  find

- *Iced tea spoon for deseeding*

  chiles such as jalapeños

- *Mechanical fruit juicer*

- *A sieve*

This salsa offers an explosion of flavors. We like it best served over slices of smoked turkey breast. It also makes a great dip for corn chips. This will keep for 3 days in the refrigerator.

2 fresh red jalapeño chiles, seeds and stems removed, chopped fine

2 fresh green serrano chiles, seeds and stems removed, chopped fine

2 fresh yellow wax hot chiles, seeds and stems removed, chopped fine

1 red onion, diced

2 tomatoes, diced

1 mango, peeled and pitted

2 tablespoons vegetable oil

1 tablespoon vinegar

Fresh cilantro for garnish

Combine the first 5 ingredients in a bowl. Purée the mango with the oil and vinegar in a blender, then add it to the bowl. Mix well.

YIELD: 3 TO 4 CUPS   HEAT SCALE: MEDIUM

ROASTED Corn AND Poblano Chile SALSA

Ah, the flavors of 400 years of New Mexican cuisine meld in this salsa that
can be served by itself on a bed of mixed greens. Garnish it with strips of
roasted and peeled fresh red New Mexican chile. This recipe will keep for
about a week in the refrigerator.

1 teaspoon vegetable oil

1 red bell pepper

2 fresh poblano chiles, stems and seeds removed

1 tablespoon vegetable oil

3 tablespoons finely chopped shallots

3 tablespoons finely chopped garlic

2 ears of corn, roasted in the oven or on the grill,
shucked, and kernels cut off the cobs

1/2 cup minced fresh cilantro

1/4 cup olive oil

1/4 cup sherry vinegar

Salt and pepper to taste

Lightly brush the vegetable oil on the bell pepper and the poblanos and roast
them over a gas flame until the skin is blackened. Peel the skins off, remove
the seeds, and dice the peppers. In a skillet, heat the vegetable oil and sauté
the shallots and garlic for 3 minutes, stirring constantly. Combine the diced
peppers and the shallot/garlic mixture with the rest of the ingredients, mix
well, and allow to stand for at least two hours to blend the flavors.

YIELD: ABOUT 2–3 CUPS   HEAT SCALE: MILD

yellow TOMATO SALSA
WITH RED HABANEROS

One great thing about chile peppers is that they come in quite a variety of bright colors. Here we match red habaneros with yellow tomatoes, although orange habaneros work fine with red tomatoes. Serve this salsa over grilled seafood or chicken. It will keep for about 3 days in the refrigerator.

2 pounds small yellow tomatoes, cut into 1/2-inch cubes

2 fresh red habanero chiles, seeds and stems removed, minced

1/2 cup thinly sliced scallions

1/2 cup finely diced celery with leaves

1 small red bell pepper, roasted, peeled, cut into 1/4-inch dice

1 small red tomato, cut into 1/2-inch cubes

2 tablespoons olive oil

1 tablespoon fresh lime juice

1 tablespoon chopped fresh cilantro

1 teaspoon minced fresh mint

1/2 teaspoon minced garlic

Salt and freshly ground pepper

Combine all ingredients in large bowl and mix well. Let stand 30 minutes before serving to let the flavors mix.

YIELD: ABOUT 4 CUPS   HEAT SCALE: HOT

GREAT SALSAS BY THE BOSS OF SAUCE

NEW MEXICAN Quincendental HOT SALSA

Quinces, which are grown in many New Mexican backyards, are treated like apples. You can find them in specialty markets; they don't have to be cooked—just thinly sliced. This salsa is much like a chutney and could be served with a rich meal like a Thanksgiving goose, or alongside chicken or turkey *mole*. This will keep for about a week in the refrigerator.

- 1 ripe quince, stem removed, cored, and thinly sliced
- 1 lime, juiced
- 2 tablespoons red New Mexican chile powder, Chimayó preferred
- 1 medium onion, chopped
- 3 tablespoons red wine vinegar
- 1/4 cup salted *pepitas* (roasted pumpkin seeds)
- 1 teaspoon dark brown sugar

Rub the quince slices with lime juice and dip them in the chile powder until they are caked with it. Place the slices in a mixing bowl. Marinate the onion in the vinegar for 20 minutes, then drain and discard the vinegar. Add the onion to the quince slices, then add any remaining lime juice, pepitas, and brown sugar. Stir very gently 3 or 4 times.

YIELD: ABOUT 2 CUPS   HEAT SCALE: MEDIUM

Variation: To make a quince dessert salsa, melt 1/2 stick of butter, add 1/2 cup of brown sugar and 1 cup of this salsa. Cook for about 5 minutes, then serve over ice cream or crepes.

All you need to make your own chile powder is a spice mill or coffee grinder, plastic gloves, and a painter's mask. Virtually any chiles can be used, but they must be completely dry and brittle. If not, dry them on a cookie sheet in a 200° F oven. Wearing the gloves, remove the seeds and stems and break the chiles into pieces. Wear a painter's mask to avoid sneezing and grind the pods into the texture of powder desired. Since chile colors vary, it is possible to make powders from light green to almost black.

Tex-Mex
SALSAS

One of our favorite salsa events,

the *Austin Chronicle* Hot Sauce Festival, occurs in Austin at the perfect time of the year–August. The temperature usually matches the humidity at ninety-six, and it takes a combination of salsa and beer to cool everyone off. What's that, salsa will cool you off? Why certainly, because the chiles in the salsa stimulate gustatory sweating, as if perspiring from the heat weren't enough.

Nearly 300 individuals, manufacturers, and restaurants enter their salsas in a competition where Dave and salsa experts such as chefs Mark Miller, Stephan Pyles, and Jay McCarthy are the judges. It is no coincidence that those three chefs have top restaurants in Austin and Dallas, where they feature their own salsas. What's it like to taste hundreds of hot sauces in a few hours? "A blistering blur," says Dave.

Thousands and thousands of salsa aficionados attend the event at the Travis County Farmers' Market, where they stand in long lines to sample the entries after the judges have tried them. Austin probably leads the world in the development of new salsas, and many of the top winners in the individual category have gone on to become manufacturers. Incidentally, there's a great sampling of Texas salsas at the Central Market in Austin, which stocks hundreds of salsas and hot sauces.

One of the major reasons for the fanatic interest in salsas in southwestern Texas is the longtime connection with Mexico. There is considerably more commerce and migration between Texas and Mexico than there is between New Mexico and Mexico, and that means that Mexican styles and ingredients–particularly chiles–commonly appear in Texas salsas. Combine those Mexican influences with innovative chefs and home cooks and eclectic salsas are the result. Many of these recipes were inspired by sauces tasted at the *Austin Chronicle* Hot Sauce Festival.

Southwestern Texas is also chile pepper country, with farmers growing many different varieties on small farms. In Stonewall in the Texas Hill Country, our friend Jeff Campbell grows habaneros, jalapeños, and New Mexican varieties to use in his bottled products, but he also sells the chiles at his roadside stand so that home cooks in Austin and San Antonio can make their own salsas from fresh chiles. Jeff was the first grower to perfect habanero cultivation in Texas, and he is one of the reasons that it is so popular in the state—and shows up in so many Texas salsas.

Other chiles popular in Texas salsas are the dried Mexican chiles, including ancho, pasilla, and chipotle, a smoked jalapeño. Because they grow wild all over south Texas, the chiltepins, called chilipiquins, show up in salsas too. They are tiny, spherical or oblong pods that are extremely hot.

Our salsas begin with one that is sometimes called "the salsa with six names" because it's often called "salsa fresca," "salsa cruda," and a few others, but most aficionados know it as Basic Pico de Gallo Salsa. Another basic and simple salsa (but high in flavor) that's very popular in the Lone Star State is Roasted Tomato and Serrano Salsa. Tomatillo-Serrano Salsa is the classic Texas "green sauce" that is served with every meal in Tex-Mex restaurants.

The appearance of Xnipec Salsa shows that the influence of Mexico on Texas foods extends all the way south to the Yucatán, as this is a Mayan sauce. Tart Black Bean Salsa illustrates that beans other than pinto beans are showing up in Southwestern foods. Corn-*Huitlacoche* Salsa with Chipotle is dominated by a tasty corn fungus, *huitlacoche*, that has a flavor that melds perfectly with the smoked jalapeños. Tropical fruits, chiles, and a tuber play key roles in Habanero-Papaya Salsa with Jicama, which is great with seafood.

Texans love their barbecues, and we have two unique sauces to assist them in their search for the perfect BBQ. Paso del Norte Barbecue Sauce, from El Paso, utilizes New Mexican chiles, while Smoky-Hot Texas BBQ Sauce features chipotles.

"Chili powder" is actually a blend of red chiles and other spices, such as cumin. You can make your own custom blend, combining a mild powder such as paprika or New Mexican, with a hotter powder such as habanero in a ratio of about 5 mild to 1 hot. To add smokiness, simply add powdered chipotle chiles.

Other influences on Texas include the *moles* of central and southern Mexico, and W.C. has created Red Citrus Mole Sauce, adding the tartness of citrus. Also fruity is Hill County Pungent Peach-Pecan Sauce, which includes two favorite Texas crops, peaches and pecans.

Texas Ranchero Sauce is the one to use to cover Texas-style *huevos rancheros*. Use W.C.'s recipe for the eggs in Chapter 5 and substitute this salsa. We complete our tour of Texas salsas with two unusual ones. Texas Gunpowder Salsa, features jalapeño powder, which can be quite hot, while Texas Gulf Marigold Crab Claw Salsa could be the most unique salsa in the book!

BASIC Pico de Gallo SALSA

This universal salsa, named for the sharpness of a rooster's beak, is served all over the Southwest and often shows up with non-traditional ingredients such as canned tomatoes, bell peppers, or spices like oregano. Here is the most authentic version. Remember that everything in it should be as fresh as possible, and the vegetables must be hand-chopped. Never, never use a blender or food processor. Pico de Gallo is best when the tomatoes come from the garden, not from the supermarket. It can be used as a dip for chips, or for spicing up fajitas and other Texas and northern Mexican specialties such as soft tacos filled with *carne asada*. This will keep for about 3 days in the refrigerator.

> 4 (or more for a hotter salsa) fresh serrano or jalapeño chiles, stems removed, minced
>
> 2 large, ripe tomatoes, diced
>
> 1 medium onion, minced
>
> 2 cloves garlic, minced
>
> 1/4 cup minced fresh cilantro
>
> 2 tablespoons vinegar
>
> 2 tablespoons vegetable oil

Combine all ingredients, mix well, and let the salsa sit, covered, for at least an hour to blend the flavors.

YIELD: 3 CUPS   HEAT SCALE: MEDIUM

ROASTED TOMATO AND Serrano SALSA

Fresh chiles that are found in markets (especially farmer's markets) are serranos and habaneros. The serranos—smaller, thinner, and hotter than jalapeños—are the classic chiles of the Mexican "pico de gallo" fresh salsas. Generally speaking, any of the small fresh peppers may be substituted for each other. Habaneros, serranos, and jalapeños can all be easily frozen. Wash and dry the chiles, spread them on a cookie sheet and freeze. After they are frozen solid, store them in a bag. Frozen chiles will keep about a year at 0° F.

Here's a salsa that bridges the gap between cooked and uncooked salsas. It's a simple but tasty sauce that's served in south Texas norteño restaurants. The texture is smooth and the sauce is flecked with tiny bits of the charred chile and tomato skins, which add an interesting taste. Serve with chips or as a topping for grilled meats. It also makes a great taco sauce. It will keep for about 3 days in the refrigerator.

2 large, ripe tomatoes
4 fresh serrano chiles, stems removed
1/4 teaspoon salt

Grill the tomatoes and chiles by placing them 3 to 6 inches above hot coals. Turn them often until they are soft and the skins are charred. Remove and discard the seeds from the chiles and tomatoes and purée them in a blender for about 30 seconds. Strain the salsa through a colander and add the salt, stirring well.

YIELD: 1/2 CUP   HEAT SCALE: MEDIUM

Tomatillo-SERRANO SALSA

When you order "green sauce" in Texas, this is what you will be served. It differs from New Mexico's green sauce in that the color is derived from tomatillos rather than from green chiles. This sauce can be used as a dipping sauce, with enchiladas, or as a topping for grilled poultry or fish. This will keep for about 3 days in the refrigerator.

3 pounds tomatillos

1 bunch scallions

1 small bunch fresh cilantro

1 tablespoon garlic in oil

2 teaspoons sugar

2 teaspoons freshly squeezed lime juice,
Key limes preferred

1 tablespoon chicken granules dissolved in
2 tablespoons water

6 fresh serrano chiles, stems removed

Roast the tomatillos in a roasting pan under the broiler until they are brown and squishy. Turn them over with a pair of tongs and repeat the process. Take the roasted tomatillos, including all the liquid from the roasting process, and combine them with the remaining ingredients in a food processor and purée.

Note: To make a cooked sauce, simply simmer this mixture for ten minutes before serving or incorporating into another recipe.

YIELD: 4 CUPS   HEAT SCALE: MEDIUM

Xnipec SALSA

This stunning yet simple salsa from Yucatán, Mexico is served in Mexican restaurants in Austin. The name means "dog's nose," possibly a reference to a salsa so hot it can make your nose run. Fresh habanero chiles are sometimes hard to find, so serranos may be substituted, but double the number used. However, the salsa won't have the same marvelous aroma. Use the salsa with grilled fish or grilled chicken, or try it over any style of eggs! It will keep for about a week in the refrigerator.

**4 fresh habanero chiles,
stems and seeds removed, minced**

4 limes, juiced

1 red onion, diced

1 medium tomato, diced

Soak the diced onion in the lime juice for at least 30 minutes. Add all the other ingredients and mix, salt to taste, and add a little water if desired.

YIELD: 1 1/2 CUPS   HEAT SCALE: EXTREMELY HOT

TART Black Bean SALSA

A mild and attractive salsa, this one works well with grilled food such as fajitas. W.C. suggests that it would be perfect with grilled quail. The cascabel chiles are the round ones that rattle; they are available by mail-order or can be found in hot shops. This will keep for about a week in the refrigerator.

Green chile is a low-acid fruit and for that reason we do not recommend canning it. We find freezing a much easier and more flavorful method of preservation.

1/2 cup lime juice, Key limes preferred

3 dried cascabel chiles,
seeds and stems removed, crushed

2 medium dried pasilla chiles,
seeds and stems removed, chopped fine

2 to 4 dried piquin chiles, crushed

1 medium yellow bell pepper, diced

1 medium red bell pepper, diced

1 onion, chopped

2 cups cooked black beans

2 tablespoons balsamic vinegar

1 tablespoon tomato paste

1/4 teaspoon ground coriander

1/2 teaspoon salt

Combine all ingredients in a large bowl and mix well. Allow to stand for 1/2 hour to blend flavors. Serve at room temperature.

YIELD: ABOUT 3 CUPS   HEAT SCALE: HOT

Corn-HUITLACOCHE SALSA WITH Chipotle

Called "Mexican truffles," *huitlachoche* is an incredibly tasty, very dark fungus that grows on corn, so it is appropriately mixed with corn kernels in this salsa of deep, smoky, and spicy flavors. Serve this salsa over something appropriately rich, such as roasted pork tenderloin. *Huitlacoche* is available canned or frozen in Mexican and Hispanic markets, and is sometimes available by mail-order. This will keep for about 3 days in the refrigerator.

1 tablespoons extra virgin olive oil

1/2 tablespoon minced garlic

1/2 cup drained canned *huitlacoche*

1/2 medium onion, chopped

2 ears of corn, kernels cut off

2 dried chipotle chiles, rehydrated in hot water, chopped

1/2 tablespoon freshly squeezed lime juice
(Key lime preferred)

1/2 tablespoon freshly squeezed lemon juice

1/2 teaspoon Mexican oregano

1/4 teaspoon salt

1 cup cooked black beans

2 Roma tomatoes, oven-roasted and puréed

1/2 medium onion, oven-roasted and puréed

1/2 cup diced red bell pepper

In a saucepan, heat the olive oil and add the garlic, *huitlacoche*, onion, corn, and chipotle chiles. Sauté for 20 minutes over low heat, stirring occasionally. In a bowl, combine the lime juice, lemon juice, oregano, salt, black beans, tomatoes, onion, and bell pepper, and mix well. Add the sautéed mixture, mix well, and let stand for 1 hour before serving.

YIELD: ABOUT 4 CUPS   HEAT SCALE: MEDIUM

More Favorite Entrée Uses for

Homemade Hot Sauce:

- *Turn up the heat in your*

  stir-fry dishes.

- *An excellent condiment for*

  burgers, or mix the hot

  sauce with the ground meat

  before cooking.

- *On the run? Grown-up*

  grilled cheese sandwich—

  fast and flavorful.

- *Why not a hot and spicy*

  tomato sauce for your pasta?

Paso del Norte BARBECUE SAUCE

New Mexican chiles are commonly used in West Texas and El Paso, where this recipe originated. Use this over smoked meats such as brisket, sausage, or chicken. Or, marinate a chicken in this sauce and then bake it in the oven, using additional sauce to finish the dish at the table. This will keep for about 3 days in the refrigerator.

4 dried red New Mexican chiles, stems and seeds removed

4 small dried red chiles such as piquíns or chiltepíns

1 cup water

1 large onion, chopped

4 cloves garlic, chopped

2 tablespoons vegetable oil

1 1/2 cups ketchup

12 ounces beer

1/4 cup brown sugar

3 tablespoons cider vinegar

2 tablespoons Worcestershire sauce

2 teaspoons dry mustard

1 teaspoon freshly ground black pepper

In a saucepan, simmer the chiles in 1 cup water for 15 minutes or until softened. Purée the chiles in the water to make a smooth sauce. Strain the sauce. Sauté the onions and the garlic in the oil until soft. Combine the puréed chiles and the remaining ingredients in a saucepan, bring to a boil, reduce the heat, and simmer for an hour. Purée the sauce until smooth. If the sauce is not thick enough, return to the heat and continue to simmer until the desired consistency is obtained.

YIELD: 2 CUPS   HEAT SCALE: HOT

Chile seeds are perfectly edible—they just don't taste particularly good. In fact, we think they add bitterness to both powders and salsas, so we generally remove them. They also affect the color of chile powders by lightening them. When you remove seeds from fresh or dried chiles, try not to remove the membranes surrounding them or you will reduce the heat of the chile pod.

HABANERO-Papaya SALSA WITH Jicama

Habaneros have hit the big time in Texas. In the late summer and fall, hab fans drive all the way to Stonewall in the Hill Country to buy a box of Jeff Campbell's orange beauties at his Stonewall Chili Pepper roadside stand. Here is one of our creations using Texas habs—and a few other south of the border ingredients. Serve this fruity and tart salsa with sautéed seafood or roasted meats. This will keep for about a week in the refrigerator.

1 medium jicama (about 1/2 pound), peeled and diced

1 ripe papaya, peeled, seeded, and diced

1 small red onion, chopped fine

1/2 cup coarsely chopped fresh cilantro

1 fresh habanero chile, seeds and stem removed, minced

1/2 cup freshly squeezed lime juice

1/4 cup olive oil

Salt and pepper to taste

Combine all ingredients in a bowl, mix well, and let stand for 1 hour to blend the flavors.

YIELD: ABOUT 3-4 CUPS   HEAT SCALE: MEDIUM TO HOT

Smoky-HOT TEXAS BBQ SAUCE

The smoked jalapeño, known as the chipotle chile, has gained such popularity that there's even a cookbook devoted to it! It particularly works well with barbecuing and grilling. This will keep for about a week in the refrigerator.

3 chipotle chiles from a can, minced

1 1/2 tablespoons vegetable oil

1 medium onion, minced

2 cloves garlic, peeled and minced

2 red bell peppers, roasted, peeled, seeded and finely chopped

2 onions, roasted and minced

3 tomatoes, roasted and minced

3 cups ketchup

1/2 cup Worcestershire sauce

1/2 cup red wine vinegar

1/2 cup brown sugar

Hot sauces are great at both flavoring and spicing up marinades, and most of the milder hot sauces are excellent marinades themselves. Generally speaking, the longer meat marinades, the hotter it will become. Poking holes in the meat with a fork will speed the marinating process along—except for steaks, which should not be punctured.

Soak the chipotle chiles in warm water until they are reconstituted, then chop finely. Discard the water. In a medium saucepan heat the oil and sauté the onion. After the onion is translucent, add the garlic and continue to sauté. To roast the peppers, onions, and tomatoes, place them whole in a large, hot cast iron skillet over high heat. Heat until slightly blackened, stirring often. In a large saucepan, combine all the ingredients and bring the mixture to a low boil over a medium heat. Let the mixture cool and then purée in a food processor until smooth. You can thin the mixture with water if you so desire.

YIELD: ABOUT 4 CUPS   HEAT SCALE: MEDIUM

RED CITRUS Mole SAUCE

Because of the heavy Mexican immigration in Texas, *moles* of all kinds are very popular. This is one of W.C.'s favorites, incorporating citrus flavors into the more traditional *mole* ingredients spiked with pasilla and mirasol chiles. Serve it over poached chicken breasts on a bed of rice pilaf. This will keep for about 10 days in the refrigerator.

8 dried pasilla chiles, seeds and stems removed, torn into pieces (or substitute 6 ancho chiles)

4 dried mirasol chiles, seeds and stems removed, or substitute 1 New Mexican red chile

1/4 cup slivered almonds

1/4 cup roasted pepitas (pumpkin or squash seeds)

3 cloves garlic

1 medium onion, chopped

4 medium tomatoes, peeled and seeded

1/4 orange, juiced

1/4 lime, juiced

1/4 lemon, juiced

2 tablespoons honey

1/4 cup golden raisins

1 corn tortilla

1/2 teaspoon ground cinnamon, Mexican preferred

1/4 teaspoon ground cloves

1/4 teaspoon ground coriander

1/4 cup vegetable oil

1 1/2 cups chicken stock (see recipe, p. 102)

2 ounces baker's chocolate

In a large bowl, combine all ingredients except for the final 3 and mix well. Purée in small amounts in a food processor until fairly smooth and transfer to another bowl. Heat the oil in a large, heavy skillet. Add the purée, stirring slowly but constantly, and cook for 10 to 12 minutes until thick. Add the chicken stock and chocolate and cook over low heat, stirring occasionally, until a thick paste forms, about 45 minutes.

YIELD: 4 CUPS   HEAT SCALE: MEDIUM

When making a gravy from roasted meats, add your favorite chiles to spice and flavor them. Dave loves chipotle turkey gravy, while W.C.'s favorite gravy is made with duck and New Mexican red chiles. Ancho or pasilla chiles work well in pork or lamb gravies.

HILL COUNTY Pungent PEACH-PECAN SAUCE

The word "vinegar" covers a wide variety of products. There are infused vinegars, flavored vinegars, and basic vinegars. The flavors vary widely by switching, say from a balsamic vinegar to a cider vinegar. Acid content may vary as well. When running across a recipe that calls for just "vinegar" it usually means undistilled apple cider vinegar—the regular Heinz standard. Taste and experiment with various vinegars to find the ones that work best in the hot sauces you're making.

Central Texas is Hill Country, which produces the habaneros, pecans, and peaches that are used in this recipe. This cooked salsa is an example of the New Southwestern style of cooking; it can accompany grilled chicken or fish. This will keep for about 3 days in the refrigerator.

1/2 cup sugar

1 cup orange juice

2 tablespoons vinegar

1 tablespoon crushed dried habanero chile

1 3-inch stick cinnamon

1/4 teaspoon ground cumin

1 tablespoon finely grated orange peel

3 large peaches, peeled, pitted, and chopped

1/2 cup toasted pecans, chopped

In a saucepan, dissolve the sugar in the orange juice and vinegar. Add the chile, cinnamon, cumin, and orange peel. Bring to a boil, reduce the heat and simmer for 20 minutes until it becomes a thick syrup. Discard the cinnamon, add the peaches, and simmer for 5 minutes. Stir in the pecans and heat for an additional minute before serving.

YIELD: ABOUT 2–3 CUPS   HEAT SCALE: MILD

TEXAS Ranchero SAUCE

This "ranch-style" sauce is one of the most popular sauces in the state. It is commonly served over eggs on tortillas to make *huevos rancheros*. Some versions now replace the bell peppers with New Mexican green chiles. This will keep for about 3 days in the refrigerator.

> 3 fresh jalapeño chiles, seeds and stems removed, chopped fine
>
> 2 green bell peppers, seeds and stems removed, chopped fine
>
> 1 medium onion, minced
>
> 2 cloves garlic, minced
>
> 1/4 cup vegetable oil
>
> 4–6 large ripe tomatoes, quartered
>
> 1/2 teaspoon Mexican oregano
>
> Salt and pepper to taste

In a saucepan, sauté the chiles, bell peppers, onion, and garlic until the onion is soft, about 7 minutes. In a food processor, process the tomatoes to a coarse paste. Add the tomatoes to the chile mixture, add the oregano and simmer for about 30 minutes or until the sauce is thickened to the desired consistency.

YIELD: ABOUT 3-4 CUPS   HEAT SCALE: MEDIUM

TEXAS GULF Marigold CRAB CLAW SALSA

W.C. invented this salsa after sleeping on the beach south of Padre Island in '69 and waking up to the sight of blue crabs scurrying about. This is one of the most unusual salsas in the book, a kind of Crab Louis without the mayonnaise. Marigolds can be grown organically in pots; the flowers should be gathered shortly before use. Use this with the Tostada Compuesta (p. 114). This will keep for 3 days in the refrigerator.

1 teaspoon Dijon mustard

1 teaspoon Worcestershire sauce

1/2 cup tomato juice

1 small red bell pepper, chopped

1 small green bell pepper, chopped

1 Texas Sweet (or Vidalia) onion, chopped

1/2 teaspoon sugar

3 large ripe tomatoes or 6 Roma tomatoes, chopped

1/2 teaspoon lemon zest

2 cloves garlic, minced

1 teaspoon salt

1 tablespoon crushed red dried chile
(W.C. uses air-dried serranos, somewhat hotter than mirasols, or New Mexico red chile pods)

1 cup lightly packed marigold flowers

16 large Gulf crab claws, meat carefully extracted to avoid shell or membrane bits

In a small bowl combine the mustard, Worcestershire sauce, and tomato juice. In a large bowl, combine the remaining ingredients and mix well. Add the liquid and mix again. Refrigerate for 4 hours or overnight before serving.

YIELD: ABOUT 4 CUPS   HEAT SCALE: MEDIUM

Unless you need a particular color, stick with white or yellow onions in salsas or hot sauces. Look for a firm onion with clean skin. A rule of thumb is that the cheaper the onion, the better it is, due to stores pricing them low when they have a large quantity of fresh ones. Do not use sprouted onions, their flavor will be off. The great specialty onions such as Maui and Vidalia are excellent when available and affordable. If nothing looks good in the onion bin, substitute scallions, using only the white part.

Texas GUNPOWDER SALSA

Jalapeño powder is available from Southwestern mail-order companies, or you can make your own by dehydrating and grinding jalapeños in a spice mill (be sure to wear a mask). Here's a salsa that's excellent for barbecues, to serve over hamburgers, or with chips. This will keep for about 3 days in the refrigerator.

> 3/4 cup "Texas Gunpowder," or jalapeño powder
>
> 1 cup boiling water
>
> 1 tablespoon cider vinegar
>
> 1/4 cup extra virgin olive oil
>
> 1 tablespoon dried Mexican oregano
>
> 3 cloves garlic, minced
>
> 1 cup chicken stock
>
> 1/2 cup chopped onion
>
> 6 medium Roma tomatoes, chopped
>
> 2 tablespoons chopped fresh cilantro
>
> 1 teaspoon salt
>
> 1 teaspoon sugar

In a bowl, combine the jalapeño powder and the boiling water, taking care not to inhale the fumes. In a food processor or blender, combine the cider vinegar, olive oil, oregano, garlic, and chicken stock and purée. Add the purée to the jalapeño mix, add the remaining ingredients and mix well. Refrigerate for an hour before serving.

YIELD: 3 TO 4 CUPS   HEAT SCALE: HOT TO EXTREMELY HOT

CHAPTER 3

Sonoran-STYLE Sauces

It may be mid-April

or late October, but the temperature is always in the nineties at the two main salsa events in Arizona. In April, it's the Hava-Salsa Challenge at Lake Havasu City, and Dave journeys there to be head judge of the competition between businesses, organizations, and individuals. They must prepare their salsas on-site, unlike the Austin competition where the competitors must make their entry at home.

In October, the focus shifts to Tucson, where La Fiesta de los Chiles celebrates Capsicums in all their glory. Although the focus of this event is on chiles, salsa shows up mostly in samples from Arizona manufacturers. Dave has attended this event five or six times and took cooking lessons Sonoran-style from friends Antonio Heras-Duran and Cindy Castillo in their kitchen and also in the kitchen of Antonio's mother, Josefina Duran, in Cumpas, Sonora. She showed him how to make the Chiltepín Salsa Casera in this chapter.

The two greatest influences on Arizona salsas have been the Mexican state of Sonora and the former Mexican territory of New Mexico. From Sonora and some parts of southern Arizona come the fiery, wild chiltepíns that are seemingly used in every hot and spicy dish, but especially in salsas. The milder New Mexican chiles, which are grown in southern Arizona around Douglas, are used green in fresh salsas and red in cooked sauces, as in New Mexico. Other chiles commonly used in Arizona salsas are anchos, pasillas, jalapeños, and serranos.

We begin our survey of Arizona-style salsas with Pima Two-Chile Salsa, a very old recipe that utilizes chiles from neighboring New Mexico. For enchilada fans, it's hard to beat Sonoran Enchilada Sauce, which features both New Mexican chiles and the fiery hot chiltepíns.

A "New Southwest" salsa featuring very ancient ingredients is Poblano Chile and Corn Salsa with Morels, which also has sundried tomatoes in it. Two bean salsas follow: Black Bean, Wine, and Jalapeño Salsa, which is excellent with soft tacos, and Pinto Bean-Poblano Salsa, which is quite colorful with red and yellow bell peppers.

Chiltepín Salsa Casera is one of the hottest salsas in this book. Two cups of it sat in Dave's refrigerator for more than a year and he was able to consume only a fourth of it. Use it with care! Tumacacori Hot Sauce also features chiltepíns, but is much milder.

Two cactus salsas are next. Nopalito Salsa with Avocado is great with sandwiches or burritos while Pickled Cactus and Tequila Salsa is best with dips.

The dedicated salsa maker will go to any lengths to satisfy his or her craving, and W.C. illustrates that perfectly with the surprisingly tasty Back Bar Salsa, which is composed only of ingredients found in your average bar!

Jicama, that tasty tuber, is showing up more frequently in salsas these days. Jicama-Lime Chiltepín Salsa is designed to be a bed for grilled or pan-fried fish, while Ileah's Jicama Pasilla Salsa is primarily designed for dipping, although we have worked it into Salsa-Grilled Steak in Chapter 5.

Arizona is famous for its fruit, particularly citrus, so it's appropriate to feature three fruit-based salsas. Apple-Citrus Salsa for Seafood combines apples, oranges, and limes with a more traditional tomato-based salsa. Tart Arizona Citrus Salsa has a wild medley of flavors, including citrus, garlic, tomatillos and tomatoes, while Mandarin Orange and Sour Cherry Salsa is perhaps the most photogenic salsa in this book.

Pima TWO-CHILE SALSA

Hot sauces tend to increase with heat as they cook and the capsaicin leaves the chiles. They also tend to increase in heat while sitting or in storage. So, when adding chiles to taste, take care!

This is a very old recipe from the Pima tribe of Arizona, hence the use of bacon fat, out of fashion these days but with a flavor all its own. Pour this salsa over eggs or beans, or serve it as a side to any Southwestern dish. This will keep for about 3 days in the refrigerator.

1 tablespoon bacon fat

3 fresh New Mexican green chiles, roasted, peeled, stems and seeds removed, chopped

1/2 medium onion, minced

3 large tomatoes, diced

2 to 4 dried chiltepíns, crushed

Heat the bacon fat in a skillet. Add the chiles and the onion to the bacon drippings and sauté until soft, about 5 to 7 minutes. Add the tomatoes and simmer for 5 minutes. Add the chiltepíns to the mixture, stir well, and serve.

YIELD: 1 1/2 CUPS   HEAT SCALE: MEDIUM TO HOT

SONORAN Enchilada SAUCE

Here is the Sonoran version of enchilada sauce as prepared in southern Arizona. The Douglas area not only has wild chiltepíns growing in the nearby hills, it also has many farms that grow New Mexican chiles. This sauce will keep for about 3 days in the refrigerator.

15 to 20 chiltepíns, crushed

1 teaspoon salt

15 dried red New Mexican chiles, seeds and stems removed

Water to cover

3 cloves garlic

1 teaspoon vegetable oil

1 teaspoon flour

In a saucepan, combine the chiles, salt, and enough water to cover. Boil for ten or fifteen minutes or until the chiles are quite soft. Allow the chiles to cool. Drain them, then purée them in a blender along with the garlic. Strain the mixture, mash the pulp through the strainer, and discard the skins.

Heat the oil in a saucepan, add the flour, and brown, taking care that it does not burn. Add the chile purée and boil for five or ten minutes, stirring constantly until the sauce has thickened slightly. Set aside and keep warm until use.

YIELD: ABOUT 3–4 CUPS   HEAT SCALE: HOT

Poblano CHILE AND CORN SALSA WITH Morels

Poblano chiles, usually imported from Mexico, are often used in Arizona salsas. This one, which might be termed a "New Southwest" style, includes fresh corn, wild morels, and sundried tomatoes. Serve it with roast meats, particularly pork tenderloin. This will keep for about 3 days in the refrigerator.

5 ears of corn in husks

5 tablespoons diced morels (or other wild mushrooms)

7 teaspoons olive oil, divided

2 fresh poblano chiles, roasted, peeled, stems and seeds removed, diced

1/4 cup minced sundried tomatoes

2 tablespoons minced fresh cilantro

1 tablespoon chipotles in adobo, minced

2 teaspoons fresh marjoram, minced

1 teaspoon lime juice

salt to taste

Place the corn on a baking sheet and bake at 400° F for 30 minutes, turning often, until the corn is blackened on all sides. Allow to cool. Fry the morels in 2 teaspoons of the olive oil until well browned, about 10 minutes.

Shuck the corn and brush the ears with 2 tablespoons of olive oil. Grill or broil the corn until the kernels brown, about 10 minutes. Cut the kernels from the cob and reserve. Combine the corn and the morels with the remaining ingredients (and the remaining olive oil) and mix well. Serve warm on a bed of greens.

YIELD: 3 TO 4 CUPS   HEAT SCALE: MILD

GREAT SALSAS BY THE BOSS OF SAUCE

BLACK BEAN, Wine, AND JALAPEÑO SALSA

This robust and colorful salsa is particularly good with Mexican soft tacos, such as those filled with *carne al pastor, machaca,* or *cochinita pibil.* We recommend serving this also with *carne adovada* burritos. This will keep for about 3 days in the refrigerator. These are party quantities we're talking about in this recipe.

2 red bell peppers, seeds removed, diced

1 green bell pepper, seeds removed, diced

4 fresh jalapeño chiles, seeds and stems removed, minced

2 cups cooked black beans

3 limes, juiced

2 tablespoons chopped fresh cilantro

1/2 tablespoon Tabasco Sauce

2 tablespoons honey (light clover preferred)

1 1/2 cups Chenin Blanc or any medium-dry, white wine

1/4 teaspoon salt

1/4 teaspoon freshly ground black pepper

1 tablespoon extra virgin olive oil

1 teaspoon dried Mexican oregano

1/2 teaspoon ground cumin

Combine all ingredients in a bowl, mix well, and let stand for 2 hours to blend the flavors.

YIELD: ABOUT 4 CUPS   HEAT SCALE: MEDIUM

PINTO Bean-Poblano SALSA

This salsa has rather complex flavors for a bean-based dish. Serve it over broiled or smoked chicken or even marlin. This will keep for about 3 days in the refrigerator.

1 cup dried pinto beans, boiled for 2 hours in salted water, then drained

4 large fresh poblano chiles, roasted, peeled, seeds and stems removed, diced

1 red bell pepper, chopped

1 yellow bell pepper, chopped

2 1/2 tablespoons extra virgin olive oil

1 tablespoon light sesame oil

4 cloves roasted garlic

3 Roma tomatoes, oven-roasted and chopped

1 teaspoon lime juice, Key lime preferred

1 teaspoon balsamic vinegar

1 teaspoon raspberry vinegar

1 medium onion, chopped and sautéed for 1 minute in 1 teaspoon olive oil

1 teaspoon red chile powder (Chimayó preferred)

1 teaspoon salt

1/4 teaspoon ground bay leaf

Pickled jalapeño rings for garnish

Combine all ingredients in a bowl and mix well. Allow to stand for 1 hour before serving at room temperature.

YIELD: ABOUT 4 TO 5 CUPS   HEAT SCALE: MEDIUM

Chiltepín SALSA CASERA

Also called *pasta de chiltepín* (chiltepín paste), this uncooked and garlicky sauce is almost too hot, but the Sonoran cooks in southern Arizona swear by it. They casually spoon it into soups and stews and use it to fire up *machaca*, eggs, tacos, tostadas, and beans. This will keep for several weeks in the refrigerator.

   **2 cups fresh or dried chiltepíns
   (or other small, hot chiles), stems removed**

   8 to 10 cloves garlic

   1 teaspoon salt

   1 teaspoon dried Mexican oregano

   1 teaspoon coriander seed

   1 cup water

   1 cup cider vinegar

Combine all ingredients in a blender and purée on high speed for 3 to 4 minutes. Refrigerate for one day to blend the flavors. It keeps indefinitely in the refrigerator.

   YIELD: 2 CUPS   HEAT SCALE: EXTREMELY HOT

Note: This recipe requires advance preparation.

You can spice up a homemade bread recipe with some salsa. After the dough is proofed, take 1 pound of dough and separate into two logs on wax paper. Liberally spread a mild, smooth hot sauce over the logs. Twist the two logs together, sprinkle with pretzel salt and paprika and then bake as normal. You'll have a nice glazed surface. Also, hot sauce can be mixed with an egg wash and brushed over the dough for a more glazed look.

Tumacacori HOT SAUCE

It's a good example of an Arizona-style, all-purpose hot sauce that can be used for a chip dip, or can be added to soups and stews. Tumacacori is the site of the first preserve to save the wild chiltepín chiles. This will keep for about a week in the refrigerator.

2 tablespoons fresh or dried chiltepíns

3 New Mexican dried red chiles, stems and seeds removed, crushed and rehydrated in 1/2 cup water

1 1/2 cloves garlic

1/2 onion, minced

1/2 teaspoon cumin seed

pinch of dried oregano

pinch of salt

2 tablespoons vegetable oil

2 tablespoons vinegar

8-ounce can tomato sauce

Combine the chiltepíns, red chiles, garlic, onion, cumin, oregano, salt, vegetable oil, and vinegar in a blender and purée. Place the mixture in a bowl, add the tomato sauce, and mix well.

YIELD: 2 CUPS   HEAT SCALE: HOT

Nopalito SALSA WITH Avocado

Arizona is famous for cactus, and W.C. first tasted it in the Sonoran Desert, after being introduced to the crunchy cactus pads by a Mexican truck driver. Forget the chips and gobble this one down by the spoonful, or wrap it with chicken in soft wheat tortillas with lettuce, tomato, and shredded cheese.

> 1 cup nopalitos (cactus pads), fresh preferred,
> cut into 1/4-inch cubes
>
> 3 ripe medium Haas or Queen avocados,
> cut into 1/4-inch cubes
>
> 3 scallions cut on a bias into 1/8-inch sections
>
> 2 fresh serrano chiles, seeds and stems removed, minced
>
> 2 tablespoons fresh lime juice, Key lime preferred
>
> 2 tablespoons extra virgin olive oil
>
> 1 1/2 teaspoons freshly cracked black pepper
>
> 1 teaspoon minced garlic

In a bowl, combine the nopalitos, avocados, scallions, and chiles and mix well. In another bowl, combine the remaining ingredients and mix well. Add to the nopalitos and toss. Chill well before serving.

YIELD: 2 TO 3 CUPS   HEAT SCALE: MEDIUM

PICKLED Cactus AND TEQUILA SALSA

This unusual salsa features the prickly pear cactus—common throughout the Southwest, and particularly in Arizona. This makes a great dip for chips. This will keep for about 3 days in the refrigerator.

2 tablespoons olive oil

1/4 cup diced New Mexican green chiles
(canned will do), drained

1 pickled jalapeño chile, seeds removed, minced fine

1/2 cup coarsely chopped pickled cactus (*nopalito*)

1/4 cup minced white onion

2 ounces tequila

1 tablespoon lime juice

1/2 cup fresh orange juice

2 tablespoons cream cheese

1 egg yolk

1 teaspoon brown sugar

1/2 teaspoon salt (optional)

Heat a skillet until a drop of water sizzles away. Add the olive oil and stir to coat. Add the diced chiles, minced jalapeño, cactus, and onion and sauté until the onion starts to turn clear. Turn off the heat.

In a blender combine the tequila, lime juice, orange juice, cream cheese, egg yolk, brown sugar, and salt and blend until smooth. Add the blended mix to the skillet and reheat over a low flame, stirring constantly. Simmer and continue to stir until sauce starts to thicken.

YIELD: ABOUT 2 CUPS   HEAT SCALE: MEDIUM

Back Bar SALSA

Stranded in a cheap motel, lacking fiery food of any kind, W.C. was forced to invent this salsa using only ingredients found behind a bar. He also calls this "Survivor Salsa" and "Quick-Fix Salsa." This will keep for about a week in the refrigerator.

> 2/3 cup V-8 Juice
>
> 1/4 teaspoon Worcestershire Sauce
>
> 3 tablespoons jalapeño nacho slices, coarsely chopped
>
> 3 tablespoons chopped cocktail onions
>
> 1/4 teaspoon black pepper
>
> 1 tablespoon Absolut Peppar Vodka
>
> 1 lime, juiced

Combine all the ingredients in a bowl. Stir with a pocket knife, serve with Fritos and a cocktail napkin.

YIELD: ABOUT 1 CUP   HEAT SCALE: MEDIUM

Commercially bottled hot sauces can be used to add spice and flavor to your homemade sauces, especially if you run out of chiles. For example, if you're having trouble finding fresh habaneros, a habanero hot sauce can be substituted at the ratio of between 1 and 3 teaspoons of hot sauce for each habanero, depending on the heat of the sauce—this is something of a judgment call.

Jicama-Lime CHILTEPÍN SALSA

This interesting salsa combines the tiny, red hot chiltepíns with that tasty root crop, jicama. It is crunchy and very attractive. W.C. advises using the salsa as a bed for pan-fried or grilled fish or shrimp. This will keep for about 3 days in the refrigerator.

1 large red bell pepper, stem and seeds removed

1/2 cup freshly squeezed lime juice

1/4 teaspoon salt

1 medium jicama, peeled and diced

1 teaspoon crushed chiltepíns

2 cloves garlic, minced

1 teaspoon minced fresh parsley

Roast the bell pepper for a minute or two over an open flame, taking care not to burn it. Remove the skin. Dice the pepper and place in a bowl. Add the remaining ingredients, mix well, and allow to sit for 30 to 60 minutes to blend the flavors.

YIELD: ABOUT 3 CUPS   HEAT SCALE: MEDIUM

ILEAH'S JICAMA Pasilla SALSA

Here's another spin on jicama salsa, this one named after W.C.'s goddaughter, Ileah, age thirteen. She prepared it under his direction to test it for this book—that's how easy it is. It's great with chips, or W.C. suggests wrapping it up in a warm flour tortilla. This will keep for about a week in the refrigerator.

Store your chile powder in an airtight glass jar in a cool, dark place such as a refrigerator or freezer. You can also use zip-lock bags, but the essential oils tend to permeate the plastic.

1 large dried pasilla chile, rehydrated in hot water for 10 minutes

Juice and pulp of 1 lime, Key limes preferred

1 cup coarsely chopped jicama

1 Bosc pear, skin removed, coarsely chopped

1/2 golden bell pepper, seeds removed, coarsely chopped

1/2 green bell pepper, seeds removed, coarsely chopped

1/2 cup finely chopped onion

1/2 teaspoon dried Mexican oregano

1/2 tablespoon grated fresh ginger

1 tablespoon sugar

Remove the stem and seeds from the pasilla chile and purée it in a blender or food processor with the water it was soaking in. Transfer to a bowl, add the remaining ingredients, and mix well. Allow to stand for 30 minutes, then serve at room temperature.

YIELD: 3 CUPS   HEAT SCALE: MILD

Apple-Citrus
SALSA FOR SEAFOOD

Tomatoes are best when coming out of your garden at harvest time. A rule of thumb is to seek out firm, deep-colored, ripe tomatoes. If you don't have a garden, buy tomatoes at farmers' markets, where they tend to ripen naturally rather than by gas, as they are in supermarkets. If you must shop in a super-market, the best tomatoes for salsas will be Roma tomatoes, as they are juicy with more meat and fewer seeds. If your only option in the produce depart-ment is a hard, pink tomato, substitute canned tomatoes in their own juice or puréed.

This salsa is quick and easy to make and features the crunchy texture of Granny Smith apples, which are grown in Arizona mountain valleys. Serve this alongside any seafood dish, but particularly grilled fish. This will keep for about 3 days in the refrigerator.

1/4 orange, cut into 4 pieces

1/4 Key lime, cut into 2 pieces

2 medium Granny Smith apples, cored, seeded, and cut into 1/8-inch cubes

1 red apple (preferably Washington State), cored, seeded, and cut into 1/8-inch cubes

1 1/2 teaspoon crushed fresh or dried chiltepíns

3 cups Cafe Salsa (see recipe, p. 18)

Combine all ingredients in a large bowl and mix well. Allow to sit for 30 minutes to blend the flavors.

YIELD: ABOUT 5 CUPS   HEAT SCALE: HOT

TART Arizona CITRUS SALSA

Here's an intensely garlicky salsa that would be terrific served over grilled swordfish. The combination of tomatillos and citrus is common in Arizona salsas. This will keep for about a week in the refrigerator.

1 tablespoon crushed fresh or dried chiltepíns

2 cloves garlic

1/3 cup roasted garlic cloves

1 1/2 tablespoons lemon juice

1 1/2 tablespoons lime juice (Key lime preferred)

1 cup freshly squeezed orange juice

1 tablespoon honey

4 medium tomatoes, roasted and blistered over a flame, chopped

5 tomatillos, boiled in salted water for 10 minutes, then quartered

12 scallions, cut on a bias into 1/8-inch pieces

1/4 cup chopped fresh cilantro

1/2 teaspoon bitters

In a blender or food processor, combine the chiltepíns, raw garlic, roasted garlic, lemon juice, lime juice, orange juice, and honey and purée. Combine the purée with the remaining ingredients and mix well. Refrigerate for 2 hours before serving.

YIELD: ABOUT 4 CUPS   HEAT SCALE: HOT

Mandarin Orange and Sour Cherry Salsa

If there were one salsa from this book to photograph, this would be it. It's not only pretty, its alive, fresh, tart, and hot. Serve it with fried red snapper or other fish. This will keep for about a week in the refrigerator.

1 1/2 cups canned Mandarin oranges, drained, liquid reserved

1/2 cup dried cherries, rehydrated in the Mandarin orange liquid for 45 minutes

1 medium red bell pepper, diced

1 medium red onion, chopped

3 tablespoons chopped fresh cilantro

2 or 3 fresh serrano chiles, seeds and stems removed, minced

Pinch of salt

Combine all ingredients in a bowl and mix well. Chill for 1 hour before serving.

YIELD: ABOUT 3 CUPS   HEAT SCALE: MEDIUM

CHAPTER 4

Tropical SAUCES

Let's start

with one of the hottest salsas in this book, Way South Salsa, which has loyal devotees at the Cafe despite its incendiary combination of habaneros and chiltepíns. Contrast it with Sweet Banana Pepper Salsa, one of the mildest (but tastiest) salsas in the book. It's designed with seafood in mind. Green Apple Serrano-Cilantro Salsa combines spectacular colors with a crunchy texture and medium heat.

W.C.'s Asian influences are apparent in the next four salsas, most of which can be used to dip egg rolls. Orange-Basil Dipping Sauce for Egg Rolls is a sweet-hot sauce, while Galangal Korean Chile Salsa is tart. For a great stir-fry sauce as well as a dipping sauce for egg rolls, try the Yellow Thai Chile Dipping Sauce. Hong Kong Fire Sauce is great served over noodles.

W.C.'s Caribbean influences from his travels and his restaurant in Key West are evident in the next eight salsas.

W.C. was using habaneros long before most American restaurateurs, and two of his first recipes with the hottest chiles of them all were Salsa Caribe and West Indies Salsa. Is Hearts of Palm Tropical Salsa really a salad? We'll let our reader-cooks decide. Fruits of all kinds are popular in Caribbean-style salsas, as evidenced by Apricot-Ginger Red Chile Salsa and Red Plum and Pineapple Habanero Salsa.

W.C. loves to experiment with new chiles and new combinations of flavors. With Tomatillo-Rocoto Fruit Salsa, he explores the fiery rocoto chiles from Central and South America, and with Yucatán Habanero and Coconut-Tamarind Salsa he combines as many tropical flavors as he can imagine. Completing the Caribbean connection are a tropical chutney, Mystic Mayan Banana Salsa, and a mustard-flavored sauce, James T's Flame Sauce.

The chapter concludes with a salsa-tapenade, Roasted Eggplant with Pepperoncini Salsa, which proves just how far you can take the concept of salsa!

GREAT SALSAS BY THE BOSS OF SAUCE

WAY South SALSA

This incendiary hot sauce is one of the favorites at W.C.'s Mountain Road Cafe in Albuquerque. W.C. says that despite its heat and the warning on the menu ("No refunds; we warned you!") he goes through a gallon of it a day at the cafe, where it's served over omelets and burritos. This will keep for about 3 days in the refrigerator.

7 fresh habanero chiles, seeds and stems removed (rehydrated dried ones can be substituted)

10 whole dried chiltepíns (or substitute other dried piquin chiles)

1 1/2 dried pasilla chiles, seeds and stems removed

2 teaspoons finely ground Chimayó chile powder (or substitute other hot New Mexican chile)

4 fresh jalapeño chiles, seeds and stems removed

2 cups puréed canned tomatoes

1/4 cup chopped onion

1 tablespoon red wine vinegar

2 1/2 tablespoons minced garlic

1 tablespoon salt

1 tablespoon dried Greek oregano

Combine all of the ingredients in a food processor and purée for 5 minutes or until smooth. Transfer the salsa to a jar or bowl and refrigerate overnight.

YIELD: ABOUT 3 CUPS   HEAT SCALE: EXTREMELY HOT

Note: This recipe requires advance preparation.

GREEN Apple SERRANO-CILANTRO Salsa

There's a wealth of tart, fresh flavors in this salsa, and W.C. describes it as a "big jumble of flavors in your mouth, mon." He suggests using it as a bed for seafood in place of pasta or rice, serving it with a sparkling wine. This will keep for about a week in the refrigerator.

1/4 cup white cider vinegar

1 teaspoon salt

1/3 cup sugar

1/4 cup freshly squeezed lime juice, Key lime preferred

1/2 cup apple juice

12 medium fresh basil leaves

4 Granny Smith medium apples, skins left on, cored, seeded, and chopped fine

1/2 medium onion, diced

1/3 cup raspberry vinegar

1 medium red bell pepper, seeded and chopped fine

1 medium green bell pepper, seeded and chopped fine

1 medium yellow bell pepper, seeded and chopped fine

10 fresh serrano chiles, seeds and stems removed, minced

1/2 cup chopped fresh cilantro

1 teaspoon salt

In a saucepan, combine the vinegar, salt, sugar, lime juice, apple juice, and basil leaves. Bring to a boil, reduce the heat, and simmer for 5 minutes. Remove from the heat and cool. In a large bowl, combine the apples, onion, raspberry vinegar, bell peppers, serrano chiles, cilantro, and salt and toss well. Add the cooked mixture and toss again. Refrigerate for 1 hour before serving.

YIELD: 4–5 CUPS   HEAT SCALE: MEDIUM

Nothing is better than pulling the ingredients out of an organic garden. When this is not possible, fresh and ripe vegetables are imperative for flavor. Fresh herbs add a tremendous dimension to fresh salsas. If you are buying herbs, look for a good, deep color. Avoid bunches with yellow leaves or light green leaves. Don't be intimidated by produce departments—carefully examine all the produce. Buy dried herbs in bulk at natural food stores or ethnic specialty stores.

SWEET Banana PEPPER SALSA

Here's a mild salsa featuring the delicately flavored banana peppers, which Dave grew in his garden and turned over to W.C. for experimentation. The outcome was this condiment to serve with light seafood dishes, especially a mixed seafood grill. The best results come from freshly picked peppers. This will keep for about 3 days in the refrigerator.

24 fresh, ripe banana peppers, seeds and stems removed, diced

2 medium onions, chopped fine

1 stalk celery, coarsely chopped

1/2 teaspoon ground coriander

2 teaspoons dried oregano

1 tablespoon freshly squeezed lime juice, Key lime preferred

1 teaspoon salt

1/3 teaspoon ground mace

2/3 cup V-8 juice or tomato juice

1 very large ripe tomato, chopped

In a large bowl, combine all ingredients and mix well. Refrigerate for 1 hour before serving.

YIELD: ABOUT 4 CUPS   HEAT SCALE: MILD

Note: This recipe requires advance preparation.

ORANGE-Basil DIPPING SAUCE FOR Egg Rolls

Because of his Hong Kong training, W.C. has a particular love of egg rolls. And since they often need a hot and spicy dipping sauce, he regularly invents sauces like this one. This will keep for about 2 weeks in the refrigerator.

2 ripe oranges

5 dried Thai chiles, stems removed, crushed

1/4 cup fresh basil leaves, packed

1 cup water

1 tablespoon vanilla, Mexican preferred

2 tablespoons shredded fresh ginger

1 teaspoon dried ground ginger

2 tablespoons teriyaki sauce

3 tablespoons orange marmalade

1/4 cup brown sugar

1/4 cup dry sherry

Zest one orange into a mixing bowl, then add the strained juice of both oranges. Add the remaining ingredients except the sherry. Transfer to a saucepan and boil for 3 minutes. Add the sherry and boil for 1 more minute. Serve warm.

YIELD: ABOUT 2 CUPS   HEAT SCALE: MEDIUM

GALANGAL Korean CHILE SALSA

Coming up with secret ingredients: it's your creativity and a love of chiles. Experiment, adjusting sauces to your palate, and enjoy! Hot sauces make more friends than television!

W.C.'s Asian influences shine through in this exotic salsa made with pickled *galangal*, a ginger relative that's also called *laos*. It can be found in Asian markets. Shrimp can be sautéed in this sauce, or it can be used as a dipping sauce for grilled shrimp. This will keep for at least a week in the refrigerator.

1 16-ounce jar pickled *galangal* shoots

1/8 cup freshly squeezed orange juice

3 dried Korean chiles, or substitute santakas or cayenne, seeds and stems removed

4 shallots

8 garlic cloves

1 cup sugar

1 teaspoon salt

1/4 cup white wine vinegar

1/4 cup soy oil

Combine all ingredients in a food processor and purée to a coarse paste.

YIELD: ABOUT 2 CUPS   HEAT SCALE: MEDIUM

YELLOW Thai Chile DIPPING SAUCE

This is another experiment using yellow Thai chiles from Dave's garden that W.C. transformed into a dipping sauce for crispy fried fish or chicken. Of course, egg rolls can also be dipped into this sauce. W.C. also suggests serving it with stir-fried chicken or with tofu. This will keep for about a week in the refrigerator.

9 tablespoons crushed dried yellow Thai chile,
or substitute any crushed red chile, such as
New Mexican (mild) or cayenne (hot)

2 tablespoons oyster sauce

1 tablespoon toasted sesame oil

2 tablespoons brown sugar

2 tablespoons freshly squeezed lime juice,
Key limes preferred

1/4 cup soybean oil

1/4 cup teriyaki sauce

1/4 cup water

1 tablespoon ground ginger

Combine all ingredients in a bowl, mix well, cover tightly and refrigerate overnight.

YIELD: ABOUT 2 CUPS   HEAT SCALE: HOT

Note: This recipe requires advance preparation.

HONG KONG Fire SAUCE

Here's a W.C. favorite that dates from his training in Hong Kong. It's served over noodles or as a dip for egg rolls. W.C. suggests that it's great with ginger-glazed duck, or to spice up any stir-fry. This will keep for about 1 week in the refrigerator.

1/2 cup teriyaki sauce

2 tablespoons ground ginger

2 tablespoons granulated garlic

2 tablespoons grated fresh ginger

3 cups water, divided

1/4 cup cornstarch

3/4 cup dry white wine

3/4 cup canned pineapple purée

3/4 cup pineapple juice

8 dried Asian chiles such as santakas, left whole but stems removed, or substitute any small, hot dried chile

In a bowl, combine the teriyaki sauce, ground ginger, garlic, fresh ginger, and 2 cups water. Mix well and let stand.

In a saucepan, bring 1 cup of water to a boil, add the cornstarch, and stir until well mixed. Add the contents of the bowl to the saucepan, the wine, pineapple purée, pineapple juice, and the chiles. Cook over medium heat until thickened, about 5 to 10 minutes. Remove to a bowl and let cool. Serve slightly warm or at room temperature.

YIELD: ABOUT 5 CUPS
HEAT SCALE: MILD, UNLESS THE CHILES ARE CRUSHED

SALSA Caribe

This recipe was concocted by W.C. when he owned the Portside Restaurant in Key West. Since that town was one of the first places in the United States offering fresh habaneros in its stores, it was natural to use them in a tropical salsa like this. This makes a great dip or a topping for grilled langostinos or Florida lobster tails. This will keep for about a week in the refrigerator.

2 tablespoons diced onion

2 cups chopped tomato

1 fresh habanero chile, seeds and stem removed, minced

4 tablespoons minced fresh basil

1 small red bell pepper, seeds removed, diced

1/2 cup chopped fresh pineapple

2 Key limes, juiced

1/2 teaspoon salt

Place the onion in a strainer and rinse under hot water for 30 seconds, then transfer to a bowl. Add the remaining ingredients and let stand, covered, in the refrigerator for 30 minutes before serving. Serve cool.

YIELD: ABOUT 3 CUPS   HEAT SCALE: HOT

HEARTS OF PALM Tropical SALSA

Here the distinction between salsa and salad begins to blur. It serves 4 as a salad and 8 as a salsa side dish. W.C. attributes the invention of this salsa to his days in Key West. The hearts of palm and the papayas he calls his "bounty of the tropics." Serve this fresh and don't attempt to keep it in the refrigerator.

4 limes, juiced, Key limes preferred

1 teaspoon large Mexican capers

1 teaspoon caper brine

1/2 cup extra virgin olive oil

2 lemons, juiced

1/4 teaspoon salt

1 teaspoon sugar

1 tablespoon balsamic vinegar

1 fresh poblano chile, roasted, peeled, seeds and stems removed and chopped

1 yellow bell pepper, seeds and stems removed, chopped

1/4 cup canned pimiento, chopped
(or substitute roasted red bell pepper)

1/4 cup minced onion

1/2 cup cooked black beans

4 large Romaine lettuce leaves

16 hearts of palm, halved lengthwise

10 papaya strips cut 5 inches long and 1/2-inch thick

1/2 lime

In a bowl, combine the lime juice, capers, brine, olive oil, lemon juice, salt, sugar, and balsamic vinegar, and mix well. Divide this marinade into two portions and refrigerate 1 portion.

In another bowl, combine the chile, bell pepper, pimiento, onion, and black beans and toss with 1/2 the marinade. Allow to marinate for 30 minutes.

Place the lettuce leaves on four chilled plates, or tear them in half and place them on 8 serving dishes. Cover with the marinated chile and bean mixture, and top with the hearts of palm. Pour the reserved marinade over all. Garnish with the papaya strips that have been drizzled with lime juice.

SERVES: 4 TO 8   HEAT SCALE: MILD

As is true with fresh peppers, so it goes for dried peppers, the larger they are, the milder. The large dried peppers, such as ancho (a dried poblano) and the New Mexican varieties, are mild enough to be the principal ingredients of sauces. The smaller varieties, such as piquin, are too hot for this purpose and are generally used as condiments or in stir-frying.

WEST  Indies SALSA

This wildly flavorful salsa is another Portside Restaurant creation, designed for use with intensely flavored fish such as king mackerel or tuna. Diners at the Portside loved it with the herb-roasted chicken from Chapter 5, or over grilled steaks. This will keep for about a week in the refrigerator.

2 cups cubed fresh mango

1/2 cup peeled, seeded, and chopped cucumber

1/4 cup chopped fresh cilantro

2 tablespoons finely chopped scallions

1 fresh habanero chile, seeds and stem removed, minced

3 tablespoons freshly squeezed lime juice,
Key lime preferred

1 1/2 teaspoons brown sugar

1 teaspoon grated fresh ginger

1 teaspoon vanilla

Combine all ingredients in a bowl, mix well, and allow to stand for 30 minutes. Serve at room temperature.

YIELD: ABOUT 3 CUPS   HEAT SCALE: HOT

APRICOT-Ginger RED CHILE SALSA

Use this salsa as a glaze for roasted pork tenderloin, duck, shrimp, or chicken breast. When thinned with a little sherry and teriyaki sauce, it makes a great dip for egg rolls or satays. It is important to use high-quality apricot preserves that are at least 70 percent fruit. This will keep for about 3 days in the refrigerator.

1 cup apricot preserves

3/4 tablespoon freshly grated ginger

1/8 teaspoon salt

1 1/2 tablespoons finely ground red chile powder, Chimayó preferred

1/4 teaspoon ground ginger

1/4 cup water

1/4 teaspoon vanilla, Mexican preferred

3/4 teaspoon fresh orange juice

1/8 teaspoon lime zest

1/4 cup dry white wine

Place all ingredients except the wine in a saucepan and bring to a boil, stirring constantly. When it reaches a boil, turn off the heat, add the wine, and mix well.

YIELD: ABOUT 1 3/4 CUPS   HEAT SCALE: MILD

RED Plum AND PINEAPPLE Habanero SALSA

"A nicely balanced, complex sauce," says W.C., "with the fruity flavor of habaneros." It is designed to be served with any type of seafood dish, but also can accompany poultry. This salsa keeps for at least a week in the refrigerator.

1 cup chopped fresh New Mexican green chile

3 large fresh habanero chiles, seeds and stems removed, minced

1/2 cup white wine vinegar

1/2 teaspoon dried Mexican oregano

4 medium red plums, peeled, pitted, and puréed to a chunky consistency in a blender

1/4 cup freshly squeezed lime juice, Key lime preferred

2 tablespoons sugar

1 medium onion, diced

1 tablespoon minced garlic

1 cup puréed canned tomatoes

1 1/2 teaspoons salt

1/2 pineapple, peeled, cored, and puréed in a blender

1 tablespoon canola or any light vegetable oil

In a large bowl, combine all ingredients and mix well. Refrigerate for an hour before serving.

YIELD: ABOUT 5 CUPS   HEAT SCALE: HOT

Tomatillo-ROCOTO FRUIT SALSA

The Southwest meets the Caribbean by way of South America in this salsa which utilizes the *rocoto* chile from Dave's greenhouse. These fleshy, hot Peruvian chiles with the black seeds have to be grown in home gardens, since they are rare in this country. W.C. suggests serving this salsa in soft tacos along with poached chicken. It also could accompany any seafood dish. This keeps for at least a week in the refrigerator.

3 mangos, peeled, pitted, and chopped fine

1 cup crushed or puréed tomatoes

4 tomatillos, diced

3 fresh *rocoto* chiles, seeds and stems removed, minced, or substitute 5 fresh red jalapeños

2 cups diced red bell pepper

1/2 cup water

3 tablespoons minced garlic

1/4 cup balsamic vinegar

1/2 tablespoon salt

Juice of 1 orange

A mango is a peach that died and went to heaven. They work particularly well in salsas if you find them ripe. Set the unpeeled mango on its end and make two slices, one on each side of the pit. The middle slice will contain the pit, and the meat will be in the other two slides. Turn them inside out and scrape out the fruit with a large spoon.

Combine all ingredients in a bowl and mix well. Allow to stand for 30 minutes before serving at room temperature.

YIELD: ABOUT 5 CUPS   HEAT SCALE: HOT

Yucatán HABANERO AND COCONUT-Tamarind SALSA

From W.C.'s days of bumming around Yucatán comes this complex and tart salsa. He remembers collecting fresh coconuts and habaneros, and these cherished flavors stayed with him for 25 years. It's great with or over broiled, grilled, or breaded fish fillets or chicken. It can even liven up fajita dinners. It will last for a couple of days in the refrigerator.

2 large red onions, chopped very coarsely and marinated for 20 minutes in 1/2 cup red wine vinegar

4 fresh habanero chiles, seeds and stems removed, minced

2 large mangoes, peeled, pitted, and cut into 1/2-inch cubes

1/4 cup fresh or canned coconut milk

2 tablespoons tamarind pulp or paste

4 cloves garlic, minced

2 tablespoons minced fresh cilantro

4 limes, juiced, Key limes preferred

1/3 cup lime zest and pulp puréed together

1/4 teaspoon ground cinnamon

5 tablespoons clover honey

2 medium tomatoes, peeled and minced

Drain the red onions. In a bowl, combine the onions and the remaining ingredients and let stand for 30 minutes. Serve at room temperature.

YIELD: ABOUT 5 CUPS   HEAT SCALE: HOT

MYSTIC MAYAN Banana SALSA

This sweet salsa can be served like a chutney. It's great with curries, and the first part of it can be used as a glaze for roasted duck or other poultry. This version calls for *fatalii* chiles, a habanero from Africa, but any type of habanero can be substituted. One of W.C.'s friends suggested serving this over ice cream! This does not store well, so use it fresh.

- 4 very large, ripe bananas, mashed
- 4 tablespoons crushed dried *fatalii* chiles, rehydrated, or substitute minced fresh habaneros
- 2 cups brown sugar
- 2 tablespoons light sesame oil
- 2/3 cup diced onion
- 2 tablespoons minced garlic
- 1/2 teaspoon five-spice powder
- 1/8 teaspoon ground nutmeg
- 2 cups fresh pumpkin, chopped in 1/4-inch pieces
- Water to cover

In a saucepan, combine the bananas, chile, brown sugar, sesame oil, onion, and garlic and simmer for five minutes. Remove to a blender or food processor and blend to a smooth sauce.

In a large pan, combine the five-spice powder, nutmeg, and pumpkin and cover with water. Bring to a boil and cook the pumpkin for about 10 minutes until tender. Drain and add to the puréed sauce. Mix well and serve at room temperature.

YIELD: ABOUT 3 CUPS   HEAT SCALE: HOT

JAMES T'S Flame SAUCE

When W.C. had the Portside Restaurant in Key West, he invented this extremely hot sauce and named it after his partner, Jimmy. It features habaneros, which were commonly available in Key West long before they were in other parts of the country. It is used as a condiment over eggs, with grilled meats, or as a dip with chips. This keeps for about a week in the refrigerator.

3/4 cup water

12 fresh habanero chiles, seeds and stems removed, minced

2 cups chopped papaya

1 teaspoon Coleman's mustard

2 fresh jalapeño chiles, seeds and stems removed, minced

1 large Bermuda onion, minced

2 large tomatoes, chopped

1 teaspoon white pepper

1 teaspoon cayenne

2 tablespoons minced fresh oregano, Mexican preferred

1 tablespoon minced fresh parsley

1 tablespoon minced fresh cilantro

1 tablespoon minced fresh basil leaves

2 tablespoons balsamic vinegar

1 tablespoon salt

2 tablespoons brown sugar

2 tablespoons minced garlic

GREAT SALSAS BY THE BOSS OF SAUCE

Combine all the ingredients in a saucepan and bring to a boil. Reduce the heat and simmer for 3 to 4 minutes, stirring occasionally. Remove from the heat, transfer to a bowl, cover and refrigerate overnight.

YIELD: ABOUT 5 CUPS   HEAT SCALE: EXTREMELY HOT

Note: This recipe requires advance preparation.

When cooking the sauce, make sure that your temperature is low enough so that you don't burn the sauce. If you do happen to burn it, do not stir it, but pour out the unburned sauce into another pan. Have good ventilation in your kitchen when adding the chiles, otherwise the chile fumes can be overwhelming.

ROASTED Eggplant WITH PEPPERONCINI SALSA

This adventurous salsa or tapenade was inspired by friends of W.C. who own the Bootlegger Restaurant in Las Vegas, Nevada. It makes a great spread for baguettes or garlic bread—in fact, W.C. thinks it's the next stage beyond dipping bread in olive oil and cracked black pepper! He'd even serve it on a meatball sandwich or over a grilled chicken breast. This will keep for about a week in the refrigerator.

1 large eggplant

Salt

3 tablespoons extra virgin olive oil

1 cup minced onion

1 tablespoon red wine vinegar

1 tablespoon balsamic vinegar

1/4 cup fresh basil (packed down)

1 tablespoon fresh Mexican oregano

1/4 tablespoon salt

1 tablespoon butter

1/4 large shallot, minced

1/2 tablespoon minced garlic

1/2 teaspoon sugar

1/2 cup minced pickled pepperoncinis

1/2 tablespoon freshly cracked pepper

2 cups tomato paste

3 medium Roma tomatoes, coarsely chopped

1 tablespoon capers (large Mexican preferred)

1/4 cup grated sharp Romano cheese

Slice the tops and bottoms off the eggplants and cut them lengthwise into 1/2-inch thick slices. Lightly salt all the slices, place them on paper towels, cover them with paper towels, and weight them down with plates. Let stand for 1 hour to remove the bitterness from the eggplant.

Remove from the paper towels and rub the slices with the olive oil. Place the slices on a rack over a cookies sheet and roast at 350° F for 1 hour or until slightly brown and shriveled.

In a food processor, combine the eggplant, onion, vinegars, basil, oregano, and salt, and purée to a paste. Set aside in a large bowl.

In a saucepan, heat the butter and sauté the shallot, garlic, and sugar until the shallot is soft, about 5 minutes. Add this and the remaining ingredients to the eggplant purée and mix well. Serve at room temperature.

YIELD: ABOUT 4 CUPS   HEAT SCALE: MILD

Several varieties of the long, green New Mexican chiles are available fresh in the Southwest and occasionally in other locations. The mildest New Mexican variety is the Anaheim, a California variety that is available most of the year. Occasionally, New Mexican chiles are identified by their grower (such as "Barker") or by a regional appelation ("Chimayó" or "Hatch" or "Luna County"), which further confuses the issue. All long green chiles must be roasted and peeled before using them.

CHAPTER 5

Salsa-INSPIRED Creations
CULINARY

For breakfast

and brunch at the Cafe, the hottest dish on the menu is the Way South Omelette; it's simple but potent. New Mexican Huevos Rancheros are made with flour rather than the traditional corn tortillas, and the eggs can be scrambled rather than fried over medium.

Three lunch specials feature chicken. Flour Tortilla "Taco" Roll-Ups contain avocados and a choice of salsas, while the Border Melt is a Southwestern grilled cheese sandwich unlike any grilled cheese sandwich you have ever tasted. The Chicken Burrito with Salsa of Choice gives the cook a number of taste options once the salsas are made.

Moving on to dinner, the Pork Tenderloin in Apricot-Ginger Red Chile Salsa is probably the simplest recipe in this book, except perhaps for Salsa-Grilled Steak. We begin the chicken recipes with W.C.'s chicken stock recipe, which is not only the base for his boiled chicken, but also substantially adds to several of his salsas. W.C.'s Fool-Proof Herb-Rubbed Roasted Chicken is not only the source of much of the chicken used in other recipes, it's great when served with a medley of salsas. Salsa-Stuffed Chicken Breast is probably the ultimate connection of salsa and chicken.

Seafood is becoming increasingly popular in the Southwest, and W.C. is one of the leaders in the region in the combination of seafood and chiles. Fish tacos are the rage these days, but rarely do they taste hot and smoky, as do the Soft Fish Tacos with W.C.'s Chipotle Salsa. Fillet of Sole with Wild Mushroom Chipotle Salsa and W.C.'s Mixed Seafood Grill with Two Salsas are so simple that they hardly need a recipe. Chipotles reappear in Mussels in Chipotle Salsa, and our most unusual salsa becomes a main dish in Tostada Compuesta with Texas Gulf Marigold Crab Claw Salsa.

W.C. learned how to make killer egg rolls in Hong Kong, so how could we not include a couple of recipes? Baby Corn and Black Mushroom Egg Rolls with Two Dipping Sauces reinforce W.C.'s love of edible fungi of all kinds. A Southwest-Asian fusion fuels Buffalo-Green Chile Egg Rolls, and we suggest some additional dipping sauces.

Our lone salad is Fruit Salad with Yucatán Habanero and Coconut-Tamarind Salsa, but feel free to experiment with some of the other fruit salsas as dressings, especially when combined with yogurt. What to serve with the salad? Why not Southwestern "Christmas" Spaghetti, W.C.'s spin on the Midwestern chili mac.

We round out the chapter with two salsa-infused side dishes, Acorn Squash Baked with Tart Arizona Citrus Salsa, and Sassy Salsa-Baked Sweet Potato.

Remember, the salsa suggestions given in these recipes are not written in stone, so feel free to substitute.

WAY SOUTH Omelette

Nobody makes omelettes quite like W.C., which is why Dave devours this particular feast at the Cafe almost every Sunday morning. If the heat scale is too high, substitute W.C.'s Cafe Salsa (p. 18) for the Way South, which is way hot.

1 1/2 teaspoons vegetable oil

2 eggs, beaten

1/4 cup cooked chicken, such as W.C.'s Fool-Proof Herb-Rubbed Roasted Chicken (see recipe, p. 103), or the poached chicken from Mountain Road Cafe Classic Chicken Stock (see recipe, p. 102)

1/4 cup grated mozzarella and cheddar cheese, mixed

1/4 cup Way South Salsa (see recipe, p. 75)

Heat the oil in an omelette pan over medium heat, add the eggs, and cook until the eggs begin to firm. Add the chicken, cheese, and 1/2 the salsa. Fold the eggs over to make a half-moon shape and cook for 1 or 2 minutes. Carefully remove the omelette with a rubber spatula, top with the remaining salsa, and serve.

SERVES: 1   HEAT SCALE: EXTREMELY HOT

NEW MEXICAN Huevos Rancheros

A great breakfast favorite at the Cafe, W.C.'s version of the classic dish usually features scrambled rather than fried eggs. It makes an inexpensive, easy brunch, although it is also served at lunch and dinner at the Cafe, where it is served with ranch beans and potatoes.

1 flour tortilla, warmed

2 eggs, cooked any style

1/4 cup grated mozzarella and cheddar cheese, mixed

1 cup W.C.'s Chimayó Red Chile Sauce (see recipe, p. 20) or W.C.'s Green Chile Sauce (see recipe, p. 22), heated

Shredded iceberg lettuce

Chopped tomatoes

Place the tortilla on a plate, add the eggs, and top with the cheese. Place under a broiler for 1 minute or until the cheese melts. Remove from the oven, pour the chile sauce over all, and top with the lettuce and tomatoes.

SERVES: 1   HEAT SCALE: MEDIUM

Favorite Breakfast Uses for Homemade Hot Sauce:

- *Huevos Rancheros*

- *Add to eggs and cream cheese when scrambling for a terrific breakfast.*

- *Spike V-8 Juice with a habanero sauce in the morning for a jolting wakeup.*

- *Smother a breakfast burrito with red or green chile sauce.*

- *Add hot sauces to change your favorite breakfast sausage into a Mexican chorizo-style sausage.*

- *Why not chipotle sauce on grits?*

MOUNTAIN ROAD CAFE Classic
CHICKEN STOCK

This recipe is the basis of many of the sauces and chicken dishes in the book. It's a classic stock derived from the French. It may be reduced further by boiling the stock longer after the chicken is removed. It freezes very well. The poached chicken is used in many recipes in this chapter.

1 gallon water

1/2 tablespoon salt

4 whole bay leaves

1 medium onion, cut in half

4 cloves garlic

1 bunch parsley, washed

1 1/2 teaspoons peppercorns

1 large carrot, cut in half

1 celery stalk, including leaves

1 4- to 5-pound chicken, left whole

In a large stockpot, combine the water, salt, bay leaves, onion, garlic, parsley, peppercorns, carrot, and celery and bring to a rolling boil. Add the chicken and boil, uncovered, for 1 to 1 1/2 hours, adding more water to keep the chicken covered. To test the chicken for doneness, pull on one of the legs. It should separate without force at the joint and there should not be any visible blood. Do not overcook the chicken. Remove the chicken, discard the skin, and shred. Strain the stock and reserve. For a clearer stock, line the strainer with cheesecloth. Chill the stock in the freezer until the fat congeals and remove it with a spoon.

YIELD: ABOUT 1 GALLON

GREAT SALSAS BY THE BOSS OF SAUCE

W.C.'s Fool-Proof HERB-RUBBED ROASTED Chicken

This is the chicken that is featured in all the Mountain Road Cafe tacos, burritos, enchiladas, and soups. It's perfect for home guests when carved and served with any of our red chile sauces in Chapter 1.

1 4-pound roasting chicken

1/2 tablespoon minced garlic

1/4 teaspoon salt

1/8 teaspoon ground marjoram

1/8 teaspoon ground turmeric

1/8 teaspoon paprika

1/8 teaspoon dried thyme

1/8 teaspoon dried oregano

1/4 teaspoon dried dill weed

1/8 teaspoon dried basil

1/8 teaspoon freshly ground pepper

1/8 teaspoon ground nutmeg

1/8 teaspoon ground coriander

The most readily available hot peppers are jalapeños and yellow wax peppers. You can stuff the mild yellow wax peppers or chop them for use in salsas and salads. You can use jalapeños—either green or fresh red—in a similar manner. Float them whole in soups or stews to provide a little extra bite, but remove them before serving.

Rub the chicken thoroughly with the garlic, mashing it into the meat with a spoon. Combine the remaining ingredients in a bowl, mix well, and rub into the chicken. Place the chicken in a roasting pan, cover tightly with aluminum foil, and bake in the oven at 375° F for 1 1/2 hours. Remove the foil and roast at 435° F for 30 minutes.

SERVES: 4 TO 6

Salsa-Stuffed CHICKEN BREAST

Your hot sauce is just too hot, so now what do you do? If you are pressed for time, there is little that you can do except to serve less of it, or serve it with a dairy product to cut the heat, such as sour cream or cheese. If you have the time, however, you can use the dilution principle. Make another batch of the hot sauce, but eliminate all the chiles. Then mix the two batches together and the resulting heat should be half of what it was. For mouth burning, remember that chile is hot, beer is cold.

Serve this simple yet delicious chicken with warm corn or flour tortillas and sliced jicama that has been sprinkled with lime juice and red chile powder. Homemade sangria is also a nice touch with this dish.

> 4 6-ounce chicken breasts
>
> 2 cups grated sharp cheddar cheese
>
> 2 cups Black Bean, Wine, and Jalapeño Salsa (see recipe, p. 61)
>
> Butter or olive oil

Lay the breasts on wax paper and pound with a mallet until they are twice the original size. Divide the cheese and salsa into 4 parts. Place 1/4 of the salsa on each breast, then top with 1/4 of the cheese. Roll up each breast and secure with toothpicks.

Place the breasts side by side in a shallow baking dish. Brush them with the butter or oil. Bake at 350° F for 1 hour and 15 minutes.

SERVES: 4   HEAT SCALE: MEDIUM

FLOUR Tortilla "TACO" ROLL-UPS

Here's what a Southwest chef serves when he's got a few hungry friends over to his house. Hopefully, his refrigerator will be well-stocked with beer and wine. The idea here is to allow guests to roll up their own flour tacos.

4 flour tortillas

Cooked chicken, such as W.C.'s Fool-Proof Herb-Rubbed Roasted Chicken (see recipe, p. 103), or the poached chicken from Mountain Road Cafe Classic Chicken Stock (see recipe, p. 102)

Avocado slices

3 or more favorite salsas, such as W.C.'s Cafe Salsa (see recipe, p. 18), Ileah's Jicama Pasilla Salsa (see recipe, p. 69), and Tomatillo-Rocoto Fruit Salsa (see recipe, p. 89)

Sour cream

Shredded lettuce

Chopped tomatoes

Heat the tortillas one at a time on a hot, dry griddle, turning once. Serve the tortillas with the remaining ingredients and allow the guests to design their own tacos.

SERVES: 4   HEAT SCALE: VARIES

Border MELT

Bell peppers have no heat unless they are a variety called Mexi-Bell, which has a mild bite. The most interesting bell peppers are the brightly colored ones, which come in a variety of shades from yellow to orange to red to purple. They are most often used to brighten up salsas and salads. The poblano, similar in size to a bell, is a Mexican pepper with moderate to mild heat which is often stuffed with cheese and baked.

This is a grilled cheese sandwich that has died and gone to heaven! And it's so easy, even a child can make it. By utilizing different salsas in the book, you can radically change the flavor of this sandwich.

4 flour tortillas

1 cup Monterey Jack cheese

4 grilled chicken breasts, or 2 cups cooked chicken such as W.C.'s Fool-Proof Herb-Rubbed Roasted Chicken (see recipe, p. 103), or the poached chicken from Mountain Road Cafe Classic Chicken Stock (see recipe, p. 102)

1/2 cup Way South Salsa (see recipe, p. 75) or 1 cup W.C.'s Cafe Salsa (see recipe, p. 18) or 1/4 cup W.C.'s Chipotle Salsa (see recipe, p. 19)

Place the tortillas on a hot griddle or in a cast iron skillet. Sprinkle the tortillas with cheese, add the chicken, and cook for 1 minute over medium heat. Add the salsa and fold the tortillas into a half-moon shape. Cook for 1 minute, then turn and cook for another minute.

SERVES: 4   HEAT SCALE: VARIES

CHICKEN Burrit☻ WITH SALSA OF Ch☻ice

As variations on this cafe favorite, add cooked black beans, pinto beans, or shredded beef *machaca*-style. The key to the flavor is the liberal applying of your favorite salsa and topping it with guacamole and sour cream.

> 4 flour tortillas
>
> 2 cups Monterey Jack cheese
>
> 2 cups cooked chicken such as W.C.'s Fool-Proof Herb-Rubbed Roasted Chicken (see recipe, p. 103), or the poached chicken from Mountain Road Cafe Classic Chicken Stock (see recipe, p. 102)
>
> 4 cups W.C.'s Chimayó Red Chile Sauce (see recipe, p. 20), Dave's Fresh Red Chile Sauce (see recipe, p. 21), or W.C.'s Green Chile Sauce (see recipe, p. 22), heated
>
> Shredded iceberg lettuce, chopped tomatoes, guacamole, and sour cream for garnish

Place the tortillas on a cookie sheet, sprinkle 1/2 cup of cheese over each and place under the broiler for a minute or so until the cheese melts.

Remove from the broiler, add the chicken, and roll up the tortillas to make a burrito. Add the remaining cheese on top and place under broiler for 1 minute more.

Remove the burritos to plates, smother with the chile sauce, and garnish with lettuce, tomato, guacamole, and sour cream.

SERVES: 4   HEAT SCALE: MEDIUM

PORK TENDERLOIN IN Apricot-Ginger RED CHILE SALSA

When basting with hot sauces, use a sauce with low sugar content for grilled items, so that the sugar doesn't carbonize and turn the meat black. Most hot sauces can be spread over meats to be smoked, such as turkey breast. In our opinion, few things are better in the world than a pork roast basted with a chipotle sauce.

Here's a double-roasted favorite dish at the Cafe. Many of the salsas in this book will work, but this is our particular favorite. The pork goes nicely with garlic-boiled red potatoes and a sautéed vegetable medley.

1 1/2 pounds pork tenderloin, well trimmed

Salt and pepper

1/2 cup Apricot-Ginger Red Chile Salsa (see recipe, p. 87)

Sprinkle the tenderloin with salt and pepper and place on a baking rack. Roast in a 350° F oven for 30 minutes.

Remove from the oven and cover the tenderloin with the salsa, spreading it evenly. Place it back in the oven and roast for another 7 minutes. Carve into thin slices. Serve with extra salsa on the side.

SERVES: 4   HEAT SCALE: MILD

SALSA-Grilled STEAK

W.C. suggests serving this simple dish with a Beaujolais and some roasted corn on the cob. Skip the butter and salt, and, instead, rub lime juice over the corn and dust it with Chimayó red chile powder to make Old Mexico Fiesta Corn.

1 medium steak (why not a T-bone?)

3/4 cup Ileah's Jicama-Pasilla Salsa (see recipe, p. 69)

4 strips Gouda cheese cut 1/4 inch wide and
3 inches long

Prepare a wood or charcoal fire.

Grill the steak until almost done. Spread the salsa over the steak and lay the cheese strips over the top. Lower the hood on the grill or cover the steak with a pan, and cook for 1 minute or until the cheese melts.

SERVES: 2   HEAT SCALE: MILD

SOFT Fish TACOS WITH W.C.'S Chipotle SALSA

One of the trendiest dishes in the States, fish tacos are now served from Laguna Beach to Martha's Vineyard, not to mention Key West and Aspen. A favorite summer meal in New Mexico features these tacos served with ears of corn on the cob and ranch-style beans.

Vegetable oil for frying

8 corn tortillas

2 red snapper fillets, cut into 1/2-inch by 1-inch strips

1/4 cup flour

Vegetable oil for frying

W.C.'s Chipotle Salsa (see recipe, p. 19)

Shredded lettuce

Chopped tomatoes

Grated Monterey Jack cheese

To make soft taco shells, heat the vegetable oil over medium heat in a skillet. One at a time, place each tortilla in the oil for 10 seconds, turn over with tongs, and cook the other side for 10 seconds. Remove, fold in half, and drain on paper towels. The shells can be held in a 200° F oven until ready to use.

Dredge the fillets carefully in flour.

In a skillet, fry the fish strips in oil until lightly browned, about 10 minutes. Place the strips in the taco shells, add the salsa, and top with the lettuce, tomatoes, and cheese.

SERVES: 4   HEAT SCALE: VARIES

Fillet OF SOLE WITH WILD Mushroom CHIPOTLE SALSA

This dish is extremely popular at the Mountain Road Cafe. It's quick to make and any light fish can be substituted, such as tilapia or orange roughy. Serve the fillets with saffron rice pilaf and a sautéed seasonal vegetable medley.

4 6-ounce fillets of sole

Melted butter

1 lime, juiced

1/2 cup Wild Mushroom Chipotle Salsa
(see recipe, p. 24)

Brush the fillets with melted butter and sprinkle with lime juice. Place the fillets on an oiled broiler pan and place under the broiler for 8 minutes. Spoon about 2 tablespoons of salsa over each fillet and return them to the broiler for 2 minutes. Serve immediately.

SERVES: 4   HEAT SCALE: MEDIUM

The rule of thumb for freezing hot sauces is that fresh salsas do not freeze well, but cooked sauces do. The uncooked salsas tend to lose texture and get mushy when frozen. To store cooked sauces, get them down to a manageable size before placing them in the freezer. Allow the sauce to cool down, divide it into small zip bags, then place the zip bags in a larger zip bag and seal securely. This way, you will have handy, small amounts of sauce to thaw for use in, say, enchiladas.

W.C.'S MIXED Seafood GRILL
WITH TWO SALSAS

The seafood served at the Cafe changes according to seasonal availability, but the combination below is one of our favorites. It might seem unusual to be serving so much seafood in New Mexico, but it's flown in fresh daily. Serve the mixed grill over a bed of rice accompanied by grilled or sautéed vegetables.

12 teaspoons minced garlic, divided

8 cups white wine

4 cups extra virgin olive oil

12 fresh black mussels, scrubbed and de-bearded

12 fresh baby clams, scrubbed

12 jumbo shrimp, peeled and cleaned

4 3-ounce fillets of mahi-mahi

Green Apple Serrano-Cilantro Salsa (see recipe, p. 76)

Sweet Banana Pepper Salsa (see recipe, p. 78)

Add 8 teaspoons garlic to the white wine in a bowl and mix well. Add the remaining 4 teaspoons to the olive oil and mix well. Add the mussels, clams, shrimp, and mahi-mahi to the wine and garlic mixture and marinate for 5 minutes.

Remove the seafood from the marinade and dip in the olive oil mixture, then place on the grill. Grill until the mussels and clams open and the fish and shrimp are done, turning once. Serve with the two salsas on the side.

SERVES: 4   HEAT SCALE: VARIES

Mussels IN CHIPOTLE SALSA

W.C. suggests serving these mussels over pasta with a little additional marinara sauce. The dish is terrific with a hearty Spanish red wine or a cold dark beer such as Negra Modelo.

3 pounds fresh black mussels, scrubbed well and de-bearded

8 tablespoons butter

8 tablespoons olive oil

1 cup W.C.'s Chipotle Salsa (see recipe, p. 19)

1 cup chopped fresh parsley

Place the mussels in a sauté pan, add the butter, olive oil, salsa, and 2 1/2 tablespoons of the parsley. Cook over high heat, turning the mussels occasionally until they open. If the mixture starts to dry out prior to opening, add more wine. Serve with additional salsa, topped with parsley.

SERVES: 4   HEAT SCALE: MEDIUM

Cold-pressed, unfiltered oils add a dimension of flavor to salsas; however, when cooking with them, take care as they tend to smoke at a lower temperature. The unfiltered items add flavor and nutrition, but that's what makes them smoke. So if you're cooking the sauce, you may want to use filtered oils. Virgin, unfiltered olive oils taste great in fresh-cut salsas such as pico de gallo. However, unfiltered oils tend to go rancid faster, so they should be stored in the refrigerator.

Tostada COMPUESTA WITH TEXAS GULF MARIGOLD Crab CLAW SALSA

Here's a casual, quick, and easy main dish that's one of the lunch items at the Mountain Road Cafe. The tortilla puffs up to add dimension to a lunch that's topped with one of W.C.'s more innovative salsas.

Vegetable oil for frying

4 large flour tortillas

3 cups shredded white cheese, such as asadero or Monterey Jack

4 cups (or more) Texas Gulf Marigold Crab Claw Salsa (see recipe, p. 52)

Shredded lettuce

Chopped tomatoes

Fresh cilantro for garnish

Heat enough oil to cover the tortillas in a deep fryer or heavy pan. When the oil reaches 350° F, add the tortillas one at a time and fry for 2 minutes. Remove the tortillas from the oil, drain on paper towels, and place them on a cookie sheet. Sprinkle the cheese evenly over the tortillas and place in a 300° F oven until the cheese is melted.

Remove the tortillas to a plate and add the salsa, topped with the lettuce and tomato and garnished with the cilantro leaves.

SERVES: 4   HEAT SCALE: MEDIUM

Fruit SALAD WITH YUCATÁN HABANERO AND COCONUT-TAMARIND SALSA

W.C. suggests serving this salad for brunch with espresso and sweet muffins. For a more elegant presentation, see the note under Variation.

1 head butter lettuce

1 banana

4 fresh pineapple slices

2 cups Yucatán Habanero and Coconut-Tamarind Salsa (see recipe, p. 90)

1 orange, separated into segments

1 mango, peeled and sliced

While processing chiles be sure to wear rubber gloves to protect yourself from the capsaicin that can burn your hands and any other part of your body that you touch.

Place butter lettuce leaves in 4 individual salad bowls. Slice the banana and divide the slices evenly into the four bowls. Add the pineapple slices in the center of the bowl and spoon 1/2 cup salsa into them. Add the orange segments and the mango slices, chill for 1 hour, and serve.

SERVES: 4   HEAT SCALE: HOT

Variation: Instead of using the mango slices, purée the mango with 1/4 cup yogurt and 1/2 teaspoon vanilla in a blender and drizzle over the top of the salads as an extra dressing. Garnish with pieces of fresh coconut.

BABY Corn AND BLACK MUSHROOM Egg ROLLS WITH TWO DIPPING SAUCES

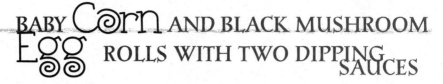

There are a bewildering number of small, hot peppers ranging in size from that of a little fingernail (the chiltepín) to the six-inch, skinny cayenne. Some varieties include piquin, Thai, santaka, de arbol, mirasol, and tabasco. These chiles appear in stir-fry dishes, are floated in soups or stews, or are used to add heat to sauces that are too mild.

W.C. simply adores egg rolls, and this recipe is one of his favorites. You can find black mushrooms at Asian markets. Be sure to soak the mushrooms before using.

1/2 cup dried black mushrooms

1 cup warm water

1 1/2 cups drained canned baby corn, coarsely chopped

1/2 cup mung bean sprouts

1 cup finely chopped cabbage

3 tablespoons grated fresh ginger

2 tablespoons minced garlic

1 teaspoon five spice powder

1 teaspoon salt

1 egg

1 tablespoon water

1 package fresh egg roll wrappers

Vegetable oil for frying

Hong Kong Fire Sauce (see recipe, p. 82)

Yellow Thai Chile Hot Dipping Sauce (see recipe, p. 81)

Soak the mushrooms in the water for 20 minutes or until soft, drain, and then chop them. Discard the water.

In a bowl, combine the mushrooms, corn, bean sprouts, cabbage, garlic, five spice powder, and salt and mix well.

Combine the egg and water in a cup and mix well.

Place a tablespoon of filling in the middle of an egg roll wrapper that has a point facing you, then fold the bottom third of the wrapper over the filling. Fold in the sides of the wrapper and roll up. Using a pastry brush, paint the egg mixture on the top edge to seal the egg roll completely. Repeat until all the mixture has been used.

Deep-fry the egg rolls in the oil until golden brown. The time will vary according to how many you are cooking at one time. Serve with the two dipping sauces.

YIELD: ABOUT 20–24 EGG ROLLS   HEAT SCALE: VARIES

Buffalo GREEN CHILE EGG ROLLS

W.C. prefers to use a bison roast in this recipe, but rare roast beef also works well. We have suggested some other dipping sauces for these egg rolls.

1 bison or beef rump roast

1 cup shredded cabbage

2 tablespoons shredded carrot

1/4 cup mung bean sprouts

2 teaspoons grated fresh ginger

1/4 teaspoon salt (optional)

3/4 tablespoon five-spice powder

1 teaspoon minced fresh garlic

1/2 cup fresh green chile strips

1 egg

1 tablespoon water

1 package fresh egg roll wrappers

Vegetable oil for frying

Red Plum and Pineapple Habanero Salsa
(see recipe, p. 88)

Orange-Basil Dipping Sauce for Egg Rolls
(see recipe, p. 79)

Cook the roast in the oven until rare or medium-rare, then remove and slice what you will need into strips 1/2 inch by 1 inch for the egg rolls.

In a bowl, combine the cabbage, carrot, sprouts, ginger, salt if using, five-spice powder, and garlic and mix well.

Combine the egg and water in a cup and mix well.

Place a tablespoon of filling in the middle of an egg roll wrapper that has a point facing you. Add a strip of roast and 1 or 2 green chile strips. Fold the bottom third of the wrapper over the filling. Fold in the sides of the wrapper and roll up. Using a pastry brush, paint the egg mixture on the top edge to seal the egg roll completely. Repeat until all the mixture has been used.

Deep-fry the egg rolls in the oil until golden brown. The time will vary according to how many you are cooking at one time. Serve with the two dipping sauces.

YIELD: ABOUT 20–24 EGG ROLLS   HEAT SCALE: VARIES

A handy way to put up chopped or diced chiles is to freeze them in ice cube trays with sections. When frozen, they can be "popped" out of the trays and stored in a bag in the freezer. When making a soup or a stew, just drop in a cube! If they are to be frozen whole (rather than chopped), the pods are easier to peel after they have been frozen. After roasting the chiles, freeze them in the form that you plan to use them— whole, in strips, or chopped. If you are storing in strips or chopped, peel the pods first.

SOUTHWESTERN "Christmas" SPAGHETTI

Here is W.C.'s New Mexican version of Chili Mac. It's called Christmas because both red and green chile sauces are used in it. Just add a loaf of garlic bread, a basic salad, and a bottle of Chianti for a festive, easy meal.

1 pound spinach spaghetti

1 tablespoon extra virgin olive oil

1/2 tablespoon minced fresh garlic

1 1/2 cups grated mozzarella cheese

1 1/2 cups W.C.'s Chimayó Red Chile Sauce (see recipe, p. 20)

1 1/2 cups W.C.'s Green Chile Sauce (see recipe, p. 22)

Cook the spaghetti to taste and drain. Transfer to a bowl, add the olive oil and the garlic, and toss. Divide the spaghetti into 6 portions in oven-proof bowls.

Cover each bowl with cheese, then top with about 1/4 cup of the red chile sauce on one side of the bowl, and 1/4 cup green chile sauce on the other side.

Place the bowls under the broiler for 3 minutes and then serve.

SERVES: 6   HEAT SCALE: MEDIUM

Acorn SQUASH BAKED WITH TART Arizona CITRUS SALSA

Here is a hearty side dish. Feel free to add such condiments as raisins and sunflower seeds, and serve more of the salsa on the side.

> 1 acorn squash, sliced in half, seeds and fibers removed
>
> 2 tablespoons melted butter
>
> 1 teaspoon ground nutmeg
>
> Salt and pepper to taste
>
> 4 tablespoons Tart Arizona Citrus Salsa (see recipe, p. 71)

Brush the melted butter over each squash half. Dust with ground nutmeg and salt and pepper. Add 2 tablespoons salsa to each half.

Place on a cookie sheet and bake in a 350° F oven for 1 1/4 hours.

SERVES: 4   HEAT SCALE: MILD

Sassy SALSA-BAKED Sweet POTATO

Here's a side dish with high-impact color and flavor. It will really dress up a simple barbecue or any roasted meat or poultry. Try it with any chipotle salsa, too.

- 1 sweet potato, about 3/4 pound, scrubbed
- 1 tablespoon golden raisins
- 1 1/2 tablespoons sweet butter, divided
- 1/8 teaspoon ground nutmeg
- 2 tablespoons Red Citrus Mole Sauce (see recipe, p. 48), divided
- 1 tablespoon slivered almonds

Preheat the oven to 375° F.

Using a sharp paring knife, slit the sweet potato lengthwise to make a deep pocket. Widen the pocket with the knife, then insert the raisins, 1 tablespoon of butter, nutmeg, and 1 tablespoon of mole sauce. Bake for 1 hour, then remove from the oven. Add the remaining tablespoon of mole sauce and bake another 15 minutes. Remove from the oven, brush the remaining butter over the outside of the sweet potato, garnish with the almonds, and serve.

SERVES: 1 TO 2   HEAT SCALE: MILD

List of Recipes

Chapter 1: The Chile Legacy of New Mexico

Chapter 2: Tex-Mex Salsas

Chapter 3: Sonoran-Style Sauces

Chapter 4: Tropical Salsas

Chapter 5: Salsa-Inspired Culinary Creations

Other Hot & Spicy Books

THE HOT SAUCE BIBLE
By Dave DeWitt and Chuck Evans

It just doesn't get any hotter than this! *The Hot Sauce Bible* takes you on a journey exploring the role of hot sauces and chile peppers from around the world, with recipes, facts, folklore, anecdotes, web sites and a comprehensive cataloging of 1,600 hot sauces.

$20.00 • Paper b&w illus. • ISBN 0-89594-760-9

HEAT WAVE!
The Best of *Chile Pepper* Magazine
Edited by Dave DeWitt and Nancy Gerlach

200 of the best recipes from *Chile Pepper* magazine, ranging from the subtly piquant to the scorch-ing. Includes original creations from the magazine's contributors, interesting sidebars, notes, quotes, and anecdotes.

$14.95 • Paper • ISBN 0-89594-759-5

MELTDOWN: The Official Fiery Foods Show Cookbook and Chilehead Resource Guide
By Dave DeWitt and Mary Jane Wilan

A chilehead's guide to the world of fiery foods, including sources, shops, and over 200 recipes. "Readers can only win with this hotter-than-Hades culinary collection." —*Booklist*

$12.95 • Paper ISBN 0-89594-739-0

FIERY APPETIZERS: 70 Spicy Hot Hors d'Oeuvres
By Dave DeWitt and Nancy Gerlach

This sizzling collection offers easy-to-follow recipes for seventy spicy-hot appetizers guaranteed to satisfy the most discerning of heat-seeking palates.

$8.95 • Paper • ISBN 0-89594-785-4

SALSAS!
By Andrea Chesman

"Dazzling different combinations...*Salsas!* shakes that sauce free of its South-of-the-Border context and replaces part of its components with those of other traditional hot sauces..." —John Thorne, *Simple Cooking*

$8.95 • Paper • ISBN 0-89594-178-3

TRAVELING JAMAICA WITH KNIFE, FORK & SPOON
By Robb Walsh and Jay McCarthy

Chef Jay McCarthy and culinary correspondent Robb Walsh take an adventurous trip across the island of Jamaica collecting 140 recipes and meeting dozens of colorful characters along the way.

$16.95 • Paper Color, b&w photographs, illus. • ISBN 0-89594-698-X

ISLAND COOKING: Recipes from the Caribbean
By Dunstan Harris

A calypsonian blend of Euro-pean, African, Indian, Chinese and Native American influences, Caribbean cooking is spicy and satisfying. These recipes represent the cultures and ethnic blends found in the Caribbean.

$10.95 • Paper • ISBN 0-89594-400-6
Over 35,000 in Print

JERK: Barbecue from Jamaica
By Helen Willinsky

"An inspired collection of fiery recipes from the Caribbean islands written by an expert on the topic." —*Gourmet Retailer*

"After reading her descriptions I wanted to grab my passport and catch a plane." —*Chile Pepper*

"Charismatic! Spicy! Authentic!" —*Jamaican Daily Gleaner*

$12.95 • Paper • ISBN 0-89594-439-1